The Great New York
Conspiracy of 1741

LANDMARK LAW CASES

AMERICAN SOCIETY

Peter Charles Hoffer
N. E. H. Hull
Series Editors

PETER CHARLES HOFFER

The Great New York Conspiracy of 1741

Slavery, Crime, and Colonial Law

UNIVERSITY PRESS OF KANSAS

Published by the University Press of Kansas (Lawrence, Kansas 66049), which was
organized by the Kansas Board of Regents and is operated and funded by
Emporia State University, Fort Hays State University, Kansas State University,
Pittsburg State University, the University of Kansas, and Wichita State University

Library of Congress Cataloging-in-Publication Data

Hoffer, Peter Charles, 1944–
The great New York conspiracy of 1741 : slavery, crime, and colonial
law / Peter Charles Hoffer
p.   cm. — (Landmark law cases & American society)
Includes bibliographical references and index.
ISBN 0-7006-1245-9 (cloth : alk. paper) — ISBN 0-7006-1246-7 (pbk. :
alk. paper)
1. Slaves—Legal status, laws, etc.—New York (State)—New
York—History—18th century.   2. Slavery—Law and legislation—New York
(State)—New York—History—18th century.   3. Slave insurrections—New
York (State)—New York—History—18th century.   4. African American
criminals—New York (State)—New York—History—18th century.   5. New York
(N.Y.)—History—Conspiracy of 1741.   I. Title.   II. Series.
KFN5696.A4 H64 2003
342.747'087—dc21   2002154107

British Library Cataloguing-in-Publication Data is available.

Printed in the United States of America

10 9 8 7 6 5 4 3 2

CONTENTS

CONTENTS

In recent years, faced with the rising tide of terrorism worldwide and its visitation upon our shores on September 11, 2001, American political leaders introduced the idea of convening quasi-military tribunals for the hearing and disposition of suspected terrorists' cases. These would proceed without juries and without the full panoply of procedural rights that defendants have in ordinary criminal trials. Indeed, initially Attorney General John Ashcroft suggested that suspected terrorists brought before these courts were assumed guilty and would have to prove their innocence. Later formulations drew back from this inversion of the conventional burden of proof (innocent until proven guilty), but the manner of incarceration of suspected members of the Afghanistan Taliban Party and Al Qaeda cohorts at a prison camp on Guantanamo Bay suggests that only the objections of legal experts prevented the institution of the harshest form of summary judgment for suspected terrorists.

Making these tribunals even more odious to many legal experts was the blatant racial profiling of the suspects. Whether in FBI surveillance photographs released to the press or in WANTED posters in every post office, terrorist suspects were literally as well as figuratively darkened in shade. An observer would have to be blind not to see the connection between skin color and presumption of terrorist sympathies, if not activities, in the campaign the government launched after September 11, 2001.

Behind the tribunals and the racial profiling was a powerful prosecutorial concept: anyone having firsthand information about the terrorist acts (that is, anyone who had heard the terrorists planning or had conversed with them) shared in their guilt. This is the criminal offense called "conspiracy." Were the crime confined to acts of terrorism, the government would have to prove acts in furtherance of the dastardly attack on the World Trade Center and other targets. Under the rubric of conspiracy, any person who was present at a discussion or planning session for a terrorist act, or any suspect who in any way furthered that act (for example, buying clothing to fill a suitcase containing an explosive device) would be guilty. Conspiracy does not require participation in the act or even that the act actually occur, and it is thus the vaguest and most pro-prosecution of all criminal offenses. This broadly conceived and selectively applied concept originated in the legal definition of slave conspiracies. When free persons agreed to commit some crime, early modern English and American law called their conclave an "attempt" and required that they act in furtherance of it to be liable. When slaves merely discussed the commission of a serious crime, the law required no act in furtherance of the offense. Mere words became sufficient grounds for the slaves' execution.

Moreover, the idea of using juryless tribunals to convict conspirators, seemingly so foreign to Anglo-American customs in criminal proceedings, in fact has a long pedigree in our country's history. African and African-American slaves were once viewed by colonial authorities in the same way that some politicians and prosecutors view Middle Eastern Moslems today: inherently dangerous and constantly conspiring; easily distinguished by dress, skin color, and speech; hiding their crimes and plots in the recesses of a culture impenetrable to the uninitiated. Slave uprisings seemed just as terrible to the master class as terrorist activity appears today. It could be argued that the slave rebellions were different since the rebels had real grievances against a system that denied them liberty and dignity, whereas terrorists cannot truly hold this against the innocents they slaughter, but this otherwise well-founded distinction begs the point. Fearing for lives and property, colonial authorities turned to mass trials and sanguinary, swift punishments, just as advocates of "tribunals" would today.

The New York events in 1741 gave rise to the most extensive set of conspiracy trials in colonial history precisely because the authorities regarded the suspects as terrorists. Unlike virtually all trials of slaves, however, the proceedings in New York City were not kept secret but were widely publicized and offered slave defendants some of the same procedural privileges that the whites accused of complicity enjoyed. The trials offer a unique glimpse into the nature of slavery in the colonial cities and how the law defined and policed the institution.

The relevance of such cases as those generated by the so-called

Great Conspiracy of 1741 stretches beyond our interest in slavery to shed light on every episode in our history where "others" are suspected of plotting the downfall of "our" way of life. This is the obverse of diversity, and it is as American as our celebrated and self-congratulatory ideal of providing asylum for all persecuted peoples.

ACKNOWLEDGMENTS

The author is grateful to Thomas J. Davis, James Henretta, Michael Johnson, and Philip D. Morgan for their comments on an earlier version of this manuscript. They were kind and stern taskmasters. Natalie Hull and Williamjames Hoffer once again put aside their many labors to help me improve my work. The editors at the University Press of Kansas — in particular, Michael Briggs, with whom I have worked for over a decade, and Melinda Wirkus — are renowned for their author-friendly approach to book publishing. Philip Koch, Keith Woeste, Vicky Sakar Woeste, and Jon-Christian Suggs gave wise counsel about John Ury's diary entry, reminding me of how difficult the judges' tasks in the trials actually were. The New York State Archives (especially James D. Folts, head of reference services), the New York University School of Law Library, the University of Pennsylvania Law Library, and the libraries of the University of Georgia, the Van Pelt Library at the University of Pennsylvania, and the Bobst Library at New York University all allowed me to use their extensive book and microform collections, for which I am greatly indebted.

The Great New York
Conspiracy of 1741

INTRODUCTION

The March–August 1741 indictments of slaves and their suspected accomplices for burglary, arson, and insurrection brought panic to New York City. The ensuing trials of over 150 defendants paralyzed the colonial government and attracted interest throughout the British Empire. What the Salem witchcraft trials were to New England and Puritanism, the alleged New York conspiracy was to the middle colonies and slavery: tests of the power and misuse of law, of community values and the absence of community feeling, of tolerance and racism in one of the empire's great bazaars of peoples.

As significant as the trials in the Great New York Conspiracy of 1741 were at the time, until comparatively recently few scholars of early American history would have accorded the cases a major place in their accounts of the colonies. No textbooks in American history featured them. In 1971 Thomas J. Davis, the editor of the most recent edition of the trial records, called the events a "neglected episode" of New York history, and in 1985 he lamented that scholars still "have paid scant attention to the episode."

Yet today no one can fail to see its significance, for diversity has become one of the central themes of American historical scholarship. Historians recognize our diversity as a nation and a people. In our past, to be sure, resentment and fear of diversity led to discrimination, persecution, and violence. It also gave a unique strength and flexibility to our country, making it an asylum for those seeking refuge from persecution and searching for economic opportunity. The British Empire of the eighteenth century tolerated diversity, but for a different reason. The empire touched all the inhabited continents of the world — it had outposts on the Indian subcontinent, the shores of the Indian Ocean, West Africa, the Caribbean, and North America. It drew from all their peoples the human labor and from the lands the natural resources that made the empire profitable. But the ministers of state in England and their colonial deputies did not embrace the ideal of legal equality for the diverse peoples of the empire. In fact, the reverse was true. By denying to the masses of forced laborers the constitutional prerogatives that Englishmen claimed as a birthright, the imperial ruling classes grew rich.

At the beginning of the eighteenth century, New York City was already a meeting place of men and women from all over the empire, but British colonial authorities in New York feared diversity. As Michael Kammen wrote in what is still the standard history of the colony, a "lack of community" marked relations among different ethnic clusters. Agents of the crown in the colony worried that it had "too great a mixture of nations."

English law in the colony reinforced these prejudices against diversity. To get along in business, the Dutch and French had to abandon their rich heritage of Roman commercial law in favor of English common law. Jews and Catholics could not use their stores of Talmudic and canon law to decide disputes, but had to bow to the decisions of colonial magistrates. Native American oral customs had no weight in colonial courts. African and West Indian slaves had no personhood in the law except when they were tried in colonial courts for crimes.

The New York conspiracy trials at first seemed to prove the authorities' fears warranted. After investigation of a series of burglaries and arson cases revealed a small circle of white and black perpetrators, the judges' fears of a wider conspiracy ran wild. They concluded that they had discovered a massive plot to burn down the city, loot its homes, and murder its white citizens. The supposed conspirators included hostile Afro-Spanish sailors and disgruntled Irish conscripts, fierce Africans from the Gold Coast and the Slave Coast, secretive West Indian immigrants and their English Roman Catholic collaborators — a nightmarish inversion of diversity. Though shrewd locals like Dr. Cadwallader Colden warned against turning a handful of crimes into a vast conspiracy — one contemporary correspondent likened the events to the Salem witchcraft trials — most of Colden's elite compatriots leaned in the opposite direction, viewing the pattern of crimes as an assault on the very foundations of their world.

Such uprisings were increasingly common around the Atlantic rim as the English Empire (the British Empire after 1707) embraced slave labor. From the 1670s through the end of the eighteenth century, slaves in Jamaica, Barbados, St. Kitts, Aruba, and South Carolina raised armed resistance against their masters, and rumored rebellions in Virginia and Maryland were quashed with great vigor. For the empire to be commercially successful, slave labor seemed a necessity, yet the growing density of slaves (constituting nearly 20 percent of New York City's population in 1740) and the increasing friction between masters and slaves made hostility between the races seem inevitable. In addition, war between Spain and England had erupted by 1741, turning a port city like New York into a potential target for invasion. Some slaves spread rumors that a Spanish fleet would soon arrive in the harbor to end their servitude, rumors their masters knew to be false but could not quell.

It would be easy — and has come easily to historians — to see the racism on display in the trials as proof, in Kammen's words, that "the magistrates succumbed to popular hysteria, Negrophobia, and anti-Catholicism. Conflicting and contradictory testimony was ignored . . . denials and professions of innocence went unheeded . . . crucial questions of fact remained unanswered." All of these accusations against the accusers and triers are likely to be true in part, but a careful examination of the law and the evidence presented at trial reveals that the truth was much more complex and, in the end, more disturbing. As exaggerated as the fears of the whites were, the anger of the some of the blacks led them to contemplate the very acts the whites dreaded. In fact, some conspirators had already begun to carry out the plot.

We have a unique window into that lost world — a firsthand account of the trials. Unlike most trials of slaves, swift, anonymous, and sanguinary, leaving what historian James Sidbury has described as "a meager documentary record, a record full of suggestive but inconclusive hints," the New York trials afforded slaves many of the same protections as free white defendants claimed under English law (only because there were whites suspected of complicity, to be sure). Because of that, there survive substantial portions of the words of the witnesses, defendants, and prosecutors. In many cases we do not have the entire testimony and in all cases we lack the intonation and gestures that accompanied the testimony. What is more, the record survives in the hand of a man who played a partisan role in the trials. Even so, the account reminds us that the slaves were neither the anonymous perpetrators nor the hapless victims of the slave system. They reappear as men and women with distinct personalities and motives.

The account was the work of Daniel Horsmanden, a trained English lawyer who sat as the city's recorder and third judge at the trials. He was a longtime placeman (patronage officeholder) and politician, and to defend his conduct at the proceedings, in which he took an active part, he compiled a journal of examinations, testimony, addresses to the court, and documentary evidence. To him it proved that there had indeed been a widespread and deadly conspiracy. His fellow judges approved the work. Our knowledge of the conspiracy depends almost entirely on this journal for the deliberations of the court and examination of suspects were not made public until near the end of the trials, and the official records of the New York Supreme Court that held the trials were destroyed in the 1911 fire at the New York State Archives in Albany.

How are we to read Horsmanden's account? Is it trustworthy? Should it be discarded as the work of an affrighted and hysterical partisan? Or, rather, how are we to decide which parts of it are accurate? Comparing his journal to the surviving legal records in the secretary of state's collection of New York's historical manuscripts reveals that Horsmanden copied just about everything relating to the court's records and included all of it in his journal. But even those documents had a spin to them. As he admitted at the outset, "The reader must not expect in the following sheet, a particular and minute relation of every formality, question and answer, that passed upon the trials." Horsmanden collected "all the notes that were taken by the court, and gentlemen at the bar," but these were the work of men determined to ferret out and smash a conspiracy. Indeed, the documents demonstrated that the judges had jumped in to examine witnesses and suspects. The grand juries then repeated the process, drawing out the testimony. Even if Horsmanden had wanted to be completely objective, his evidence had already been tainted by the manner of its compilation.

Moreover, by 1744, he had an additional motive to spin the story. He wanted to defend the actions of the court, of which he was a leading member, and the political clique that ran the colony against a growing chorus of objections that he and the court had become (if they were not from the start) credulous: "There had been some wanton, wrong-headed persons amongst us, who took the liberty to arraigning the justice of the proceedings, and set up their private

4   { *The Great New York Conspiracy of 1741* }

opinions in superiority to the court and grand jury." Although it took him three years to finish his account, he advertised for "subscribers" (advance purchasers) to the published journal in 1742. But by 1744 he had time to figure out how to spin the tale. His original title was "A Journal of the proceedings in the detection of the conspiracy, formed by some white people in conjunction with several Negroe and other slaves, for burning the city of New-York, and murdering the inhabitants thereof . . . Together with a narrative of the tryals, condemnations, executions, [and] behaviour of the several criminals," a blatant attempt to convince readers of the severity and portent of the events — and, by implication, what every white New Yorker owed to the judges. Responding to the chorus of scoffers who denied that a conspiracy existed, Horsmanden rejoined, "They could not be judges of such matters, [though] they declared with no small assurance (notwithstanding what we *saw* with our eyes and *heard* with our ears) that there was no conspiracy. . . . Those who had not the opportunity of *seeing* and *hearing*" could not understand how terrifying the events were or how they taught that "for every one who has negroes, to keep a very watchful eye over them."

For us, Horsmanden's *Journal of the Proceedings* in the New York conspiracy reads a little differently. Even the title portrays a time of anxiety, oppression, anger, and resistance in which the authorities may have easily exaggerated what the slaves and their white confederates actually planned to do. Its author's claim to firsthand knowledge must thus be weighed against his own partisan purposes in keeping a journal. To be sure, one faces the same problem when reading all official records of cases of slave rebellions. Although they purport to be accurate, they are always biased in favor of the prosecution if for no other reason than the fact that the prosecution writes them. But that is not all: the official accounts invariably justify the trial and punishment of the accused. They reassure the free reader that all will be well in the future, that the state can be trusted to keep order, that the culprits are all in custody, and that justice will be served.

In the past, historians have relied on these official records, acknowledging the biases but accepting the basic narrative as true. For example, James Sidbury reads multiple meanings into the text of the official records relating to Gabriel's rebellion, in Richmond, Virginia, during the summer of 1800. But he trusts it as a primary source. Douglas R. Egerton, Edward A. Pearson, and David Robertson do the same in their accounts of the Denmark Vesey plot in Charleston, South Carolina, in 1822. Winthrop Jordan has concluded from fragments of coerced slave testimony that there was a planned rebellion in the Second Creek area of the Mississippi Delta, during the summer of 1861.

Recently historian Michael Johnson raised serious questions about the reliability of an official record. In the published account of testimony in the so-called Vesey cases, Johnson found major discrepancies between the notes of the examinations of slaves taken on the spot and those later published by the state legislature. From these discrepancies Johnson concluded that the official, published record could not be trusted and that the conspiracy might never have existed. Slaves were coerced into making accusations against other slaves, and the city intendant was so eager to punish certain slaves and embarrass certain political opponents that he put words in the mouths of the witnesses and confessors. With Johnson's masterful deconstruction of the Vesey record in hand, one may well worry about the veracity of Horsmanden's account.

Of course, New York City in 1741 was different from Charleston in 1822 in many crucial respects. New York City was over 80 percent white, whereas Charleston had a black majority. In 1741 the institution of slavery was not under attack to any significant degree. By 1822 strong opposition to slavery had appeared throughout the English-speaking world, and slavery had been abolished in much of the northern United States. There was thus far more reason for Charleston city officials to fabricate a conspiracy, or at least to be paranoid about one, than colonial New York City's judges. Finally, Denmark Vesey never admitted or confessed his complicity in any plot, much less one to kill all the whites in the city, reduce it to ashes, and lead an exodus of freed slaves anywhere. The supposed chief slave conspirators in New York did confess their guilt — albeit with the faggots already sizzling around the stakes on which they were to be immolated.

Still, one must ask whether Horsmanden fabricated his record to demonstrate the existence of a slave plot that had no basis in real-

6   { *The Great New York Conspiracy of 1741* }

ity. I think not. The crimes of burglary and arson alleged at the start of the investigation actually occurred. The court very likely uncovered and punished the perpetrators. Did Horsmanden slant his account of the effectiveness of the magistrates in uncovering the culprits? Surely he must have, for he was a spokesman for those responsible for maintaining public order. Did Horsmanden and the other judges go too far in seeing behind the burglary and arson rings a larger, more sinister plot to burn down the city and rid the colony of slavery by force? That is what the reader must decide.

Even if one were to accept Horsmanden's compilation as a good faith surrogate for a trial transcript, the question still remains whether the entire proceeding had an ulterior purpose. Were the indictments and trials a way for the authorities to deflect or hide seething class and ethnic animosities among whites? By uniting all ranks and persuasions among the free population against the alleged conspiracy of slaves, ongoing resentment over the unequal distribution of wealth among the poor could be massaged by offering poor whites a partnership in the alliance against the blacks. Were the trials also a way of healing rifts among the elite? Long-standing partisan quarrels had split the colonial ruling class into rival cliques, but leaders from all factions were invited to take part in the prosecution of the conspiracy cases. Finally, was the spectacle of trial and punishment a way of distracting the city's population from the vicissitudes and uncertainties of the war against Spain? That war had already cost New York many of its young men, and so long as it raged the port of New York City was vulnerable to attack.

Horsmanden's motives and abilities as a documentarian do not constitute the only concern about the reliability of his account as a primary source, for he quotes others in addition to reporting his own findings. Take Mary Burton, a sixteen-year-old servant girl with an axe to grind against her master, tavern keeper John Hughson. More than half of the population of the colonies were "bound" in service as apprentices, servants, and slaves. A significant number of these men and women would either protest their treatment in some way during the course of their service or run away, demonstrating that servants were not generally a contented lot. Is Burton's servile condition a reason to suspect her veracity? She claimed to have witnessed many of the crucial scenes of the conspiracy. She was well placed to observe what went on, but did she understand it? Were words put in her mouth by the judges, eager as they were to gain firsthand evidence against Hughson and the crew of slaves that met at his establishment? Did she fabricate events in order to earn the monetary reward that the lieutenant governor of the colony offered to all informants? Even if she thought she was telling the truth, did Horsmanden accurately record what she said? Did the judges and jurors at trial put the correct interpretation on her testimony? These questions are not so different from those faced by modern triers of fact in criminal cases. But the reader cannot watch and listen as Mary Burton testifies, as jurors can today. Slaves supposedly present at the gatherings at Hughson's tavern confirmed much of Burton's testimony, but they had reasons to lie that exceeded hers. Their lives depended on the mercy of the court, and the judges had made it plain that only the right sort of confession would gain their approval.

Finally, there is the matter of physical corroboration of the conspiracy. Armed with this, one might feel far more confident of the veracity of both Horsmanden and his witnesses' testimony. Of course, physical evidence can be manufactured after the fact as easily as confessions of guilt can be coerced. The prosecution could produce physical evidence of the burglaries and of the arson, but the conspiracy consisted of mere words. The only confirmation of the latter was more words, and sorting truth from falsehood was the main problem from the outset.

A modern defense counsel transported back in time to argue for the accused might say that if any portion of the record is suspect, the jury should disregard all of it. If it does not fit, the jury should acquit. That may be the measure of "beyond a reasonable doubt," and one might be tempted to accede to it. Then one could accuse Horsmanden and his comrades of manufacturing a conspiracy, part of the racist self-fulfilling prophecy of white moral superiority over black.

Historians and readers of history must employ a different standard of proof. If the preponderance of evidence seems to support a point, if it is more likely than not, we should credit it. Thus, with all due concern about the veracity of the surviving records notwithstanding, I have concluded that much of what Horsmanden writes is likely to be at least partially true. For all his prejudices and the inherent complications in his journal, Horsmanden has offered us

8

a chance to view these trials from the inside. He did not hide his partiality, and that allows us to measure what he reports against what we know to be his biases. In the following pages, when his view is not corroborated by others in the testimony or by another source entirely, I have regarded it with caution and warn the reader of my concerns. When a piece of evidence he offers is widely corroborated, I treat it as a matter of fact. After all, as Joseph Heller's fine novel *(Something Happened)* reminds us, behind all the screens of bias and flawed perception, something actually happened.

Faced with a choice between a distant, dispassionate, analytical reordering of the events, second-guessing everything that Horsmanden says and everything that he tells us others said, and a narrative that attempts to convey the confusion and fear, the mutual misunderstandings and suspicions of all involved, I elected the latter approach. Where necessary, I interrupt the narrative to offer my own views, to explain technical matters, to introduce characters and corollary plot lines, and to speculate a little bit on what we might learn if more sources come to light. I have tried not to substitute my judgment of events for the reader's.

In addition, I have adopted two conventions in furtherance of narrative clarity and in fairness to all the participants. Both concern the names of the slaves. First, I have given slaves who had only a first name a last name based on their owner's. There were eight "Caesar"s, six "Cato"s, and two "Prince"s accused in the course of the conspiracy. Other historians, following Horsmanden, have tried to resolve the confusion by naming slaves as a master's possessions — for example, John Varick's Caesar. I believe that this convention demeans the individuals involved. In later years some slaves would take their master's last names as their own. I have simply accelerated this process. Second, rather than mentioning a few slaves whose cases have analytical interest, I have included the name of every slave who stood trial, gave evidence, or was found not culpable by a grand jury. If they have no other, this is their memorial.

I had intended to title this book "These Enemies of Their Own Household," a phrase from Horsmanden's introduction. It expresses his bewilderment and dismay that slaves could so easily plot the betrayal of their masters' lives and fortunes when, to his mind, their masters were the most lenient and indulgent in the world. Inadvertently, the phrase captured the ironies at the heart of both slavery and slave law. Slaves were in but not of the household, privy to its most intimate secrets, sometimes even lovers and childbearers to their masters and their masters' children, but that same slave law drew a distinction between them and their masters that denied to the slave what the free person took for granted. No exertion, no loyalty, no achievement could in and of itself gain the slave advancement beyond his station. According to the law, slaves were chattel — property that could be bought and sold freely — yet masters expected that slaves would be faithful to the household, as though the law recognized the personality of the individual slave. Such persistent and profound ironies, multiplied every day of the slave's service by the cruel calculus of oppression, could easily turn the slave into the enemy of his own household.

CHAPTER I

Slavery and Slave Law in the Early English Empire

Examined from a distance, it would appear that slavery and law were inextricably linked in the English colonies. Slave law surfaced in every English New World colony and slavery was a highly profitable, even essential, form of labor in many of them. One might thus conclude that slave law was a long-lived part of English law, carried by the emigrants to the New World. Nothing could be further from the truth. Although the connection between slavery and law would prove to be a hardy one and would benefit both the white colonists and the home country, in fact it was anything but automatic.

Although many in England were bound to labor as servants, apprentices, and contract workers, there were no slaves in England. None were brought from England to its colonies. Nor were there slaves in the English colonies waiting to serve the immigrants. Slaves had to be imported from outside the colonies. Moreover, there was no provision for chattel slavery (that is, slavery in which the slave is regarded as personal property rather than a human being) in the English common law (the decisions of England's courts), the statutes of Parliament, the equity rulings of England's chancellors, or the charters the English crown gave to companies, proprietors, or any of its colonizers.

True, Elizabethan and Jacobean Parliaments in England had passed a wide range of economic regulations, in part designed to ensure that everyone worked. Beginning in 1576, Poor Laws provided that parishes did not have to support the wandering poor but could order them returned to their home counties. In addition, the law set up poorhouses where unemployed men and women were forced to work for their keep. But such laws did not reduce the impoverished to the status of chattel. The sale of slaves was legal in England, but slaves brought there could walk away from their masters because no English law reduced them to the status of chattel. In *Somerset v. Stewart* (1772), Chief Justice William Murray, Lord Mansfield, opined that slavery could only exist where positive law established it, and England had no such laws.

Though their color marked Africans and African Americans as slaves in the colonies, color did not predicate slavery in England. The English might regard the color black as a sign of evil and death and see the African as naturally inferior to the European, but these prejudices did not lead to an English law of slavery. As London justice of the peace and author Sir John Fielding wrote in 1768, the law "had nothing to do with blacks but when they offend against the law, by the commission of fraud, felony, or breach of the peace." In other words, blacks would be regarded as subjects of the crown like any other subjects of the crown living in England.

The tie between slavery and slave law in the colonies depended upon the English colonists' purchase or capture of slaves and the enactment of specific colonial legislative and judicial provisions (sometimes called "positive" or "domestic" law) to control those slaves. Indeed, it can be said that two of the major preoccupations and achievements (if this is the right word) of colonial leaders were the development of a complex system of laws governing slavery and the deployment of the slave labor system. One was not possible without the other. Neither project was dictated by the colonists' English masters, although in time influential people in England would grasp the advantages of the slave labor system and the slave trade, making it profitable for themselves as well as for the colonists. The credit for slavery and slave law in the English colonies belongs to the colonists themselves.

Slavery was one of a number of areas in which colonial law diverged from that of the home country. In fact, legal scholars have not credited the extent to which the law of slavery in the early English colonies anticipated many modern aspects of business law. Most legal scholars place the rise of pro-business concepts of property and commerce in the late eighteenth or early nineteenth centuries. True, it was then that increased financial and industrial activity in national and international marketplaces seemed to dictate that the law favor economic growth over older ideas of fairness. But slave law anticipated these shifts in the direction of freer buying and selling of property. For example, although the relationship of the slave to the master was a traditional one — the slave was a bound member of the household — the sale of slaves was based on progressive ideas of contract. Indeed, it can be argued that antebellum southern laws on slavery survived the attack of abolitionists in this period precisely because business transactions involving slaves had introduced many of the legal concepts northern businessmen and factory owners were adopting to defend their own activities.

As innovative and effective as colonial slave law would prove, it was filled with stark contradictions. First, the law mandated that slaves' everyday life be closely watched, but slaves were not protected by the law against their masters' indifference, neglect, or intentional cruelty, a dichotomy explained by the central fact of slave law: it was not enacted for the benefit of slaves but rather for their masters. Slaves were objects in the law, not the object of it. Plainly, in the words of an antebellum South Carolina judge, a slave was an object "in a compact between his rulers." Second, slaves were regarded as a form of property in the law; technically speaking, they had no "personhood" in law, but when slaves committed crimes they were treated as human beings with the power to choose between good and evil and the will to make decisions. Lastly, the law treated all slaves as though there were no individual differences among them. They were a category rather than a collectivity of individuals. But masters and slaves knew better. Some slaves were valuable and prized, while others were regarded with dismay or contempt by their masters and coworkers. One can find many cases of masters interceding on behalf of valued slaves accused of crimes or hiding slaves from the reach of the courts.

In a remarkable example of circular reasoning, after developing slave codes to protect their investment in the bondsmen and women, English colonial apologists for slavery offered the legal regime they had enacted as a positive defense of slavery. To be sure, not all defenses of slavery were legalistic. Some were frankly based on racial animus or prejudice, while others were cloaked in biblical or pseudo-scientific language. But the legal justification of slavery was especially cunning, for it characterized the slave laws as paternalistic efforts to protect inferior beings against mistreatment. Such arguments implied that the colonists had not really created a legal category where none, in English law, had before existed. Instead, the legalistic defense of slavery rested upon the sly supposition that the colonial law of slavery was a natural outgrowth of slavery itself.

One can find this self-serving argument as early as 1664 in the slave laws enacted by the sugar plantation owners who ruled English Jamaica. They intoned the following, with utter seriousness: "Yet we well know by the right rule of reason and order we are not to leave [the slaves] to the arbitrary cruel and outrageous will of every evil disposed person, but so far to protect them as we do many other goods and chattels and also somewhat further as being created men though without the knowledge of God in the world." This argument would echo down the centuries and find a place in the pro-slavery treatises published in the years before the Civil War. Slavery in a Christian environment was a blessing for the slave; benign masters and stern but fair laws protected slaves from the wanton barbarities of other nations' laws (presumably England's Spanish and French rivals in the imperial amphitheater of the Caribbean) and other colonial masters.

But how did the law of slavery spread throughout the American colonial empire without any precedent in the common law of England, its statutory pronouncements, or the colonial charters? There are two keys to solving this riddle. The first lies in the innovative nature of the English colonial slave law. The very fact that it had no precedent or standing in English law allowed colonial slave law to develop. To borrow an explanatory device from modern evolutionary biology, it is in relatively isolated populations of peoples and ideas that innovation can best flourish. In isolation the novel idea does not have to throw off so much of the burden of tradition. In England the weight of authority prevented the development of slave law. In the colonies, where few English-trained lawyers ventured and the courts were far simpler than in the home country, there was room for legal innovations like slavery.

Why did the colonists gravitate to the particular legal innovation of slave law? Some scholars, following the work of Oscar and Mary Handlin in 1950, which itself resuscitated much older scholarship, believe that the first Africans put to labor in the English colonies were treated more like indentured servants than chattel slaves. Indentured servitude had long been protected by English law. Indentured servants were men and women who had contracted their labor for a specific time to pay for their travel to the colonies. After a term of several years, during which their masters were legally obligated to feed, clothe, and train them, the indentured servant was free. But even if this story line were correct (and most recent scholarship disputes it), it begs the question. If the first settlers had no legal provisions for enslaving Africans, and if the first Africans were not true slaves, where did the law of slavery come from?

Perhaps the English colonists simply borrowed it from their colonial neighbors, the French, Portuguese, and Spanish? To be sure, slavery was already an old institution in the Mediterranean region and Africa when the English established their colonies in the Americas. The Portuguese and Spanish slave trade to the Americas had been thriving for over a hundred years before the first Africans were transported to the first English colonies. Iberian legal authorities produced treatises defending the slave trade and the use of slave labor on plantations. Thus, one could infer that the English law of slavery was mimetic in the sense that it mimicked other nations' laws and hence derived its authority from them.

The mimetic thesis would appear plausible were it not for the fact that, when it finally did appear in the seventeenth century, the English colonial law of slavery differed in two important respects from the laws of its European rivals in the Americas. First, while the Spanish, Portuguese, and, to a lesser extent, Dutch based their notions of slave law on classical Roman sources, the English colonial slave law rejected Roman precedents. Roman law left slavery the sole concern of the masters. That is, except for matters of keeping the peace and collecting taxes, the Roman legal authorities did not care what the master did with his slave. The master could free a slave (and some freed slaves rose to great power in ancient Rome) or treat the slave with cruelty. The law intervened when slaves endangered their masters (for example, all slaves were put to death in a household when one struck a master) but otherwise abstained from detailed slave codes. The English did not adopt Roman law in general and, in particular, did not accept the Roman law's approach to slavery. Instead, English colonial slave law told masters what they could and could not do with their slaves.

Second, English colonial law did not permit the intercession of the church in favor of the slave. In the Spanish, Portuguese, and French colonies, the Roman Catholic Church convinced the imperial rulers that slaves had souls and thus had to be protected from flagrantly abusive masters. The church made a major effort to convert slaves and required that Christianized slaves be treated with humanity. In these colonies Roman Catholic missionaries intervened to protect individual slaves. Masters, influenced by the church, allowed priests to officiate at slave marriages and funerals. The Inquisition in these colonies investigated slaves' complaints against masters. No comparable religious mitigation of the rigors of slavery took place in the English colonies. Individual ministers and missionaries might attempt to convert slaves and preach to masters about better treatment of their bondsmen and women, but the law did not allow Protestant ministers to defend a slave against a master.

It is necessary to use the second key, which lies outside of the law itself, to solve the puzzle. As historian David Brion Davis has noted, slavery often marked the economic takeoff of a colonial society. Slaves provided the cheap labor that enabled large-scale capital enterprises like sugar cultivation to earn great profits. Herbert Klein has documented how the European trade in slaves after 1500 enabled European nations to grow wealthy from the staple production of their colonies. Given this economic precondition, it was in a way natural and reasonable that the importers and employers of slaves in the Americas looked to law to protect what the market had accomplished.

That is just what happened. The masters of slaves in the English colonies, living in relative isolation from the legal institutions of the home country, introduced and elaborated slave codes. Prompting the establishment of slave law was the allure of the riches to be gained from staple crop production. The British Empire before 1776 became the greatest of its time because of the wealth that the sugar islands of the West Indies, the rice country of coastal South Carolina, and the tobacco plantations of the Chesapeake produced. Although indentured servants, transported convicts, and free persons of color contributed their labor to this agricultural success story, there were simply not enough of them to plant and harvest the staple crops. Moreover, who would willingly engage in back-breaking sugarcane agriculture in the tropical inferno of Barbados, or rice cultivation in the malarial low country of South Carolina, or tobacco growing in the typhoid-ridden tidewaters of the Chesapeake without the promise of riches? Most of the labor that made the English Empire great came from the African and African-American slave because that is where the labor could be found.

At its inception as at its core, slave law embodied the self-interest of the planter-legislator. The purpose of slave law was not justice or even fairness but rather the absolute dominion of the master over his property. The process by which this economic self-interest turned into law can be seen in the first of the comprehensive English colonial slave laws — the "black code" of the sugar island of Barbados, the jewel in the crown of the seventeenth-century English Empire.

——————

To the planters of Barbados in the 1650s and 1660s — the period when the sugar industry was becoming the most profitable in the world and the dependence of the sugar plantations on slavery had become a fact of life — fell the task of simultaneously developing and justifying slave law. As the numbers of their slaves tripled every decade from the 1640s through the 1680s, the sugar planters who sat in the Barbados assembly had to find some way to make the existence of chattel slavery appear legal. In this they faced a double obstacle. Not only was there no precedent for slavery under English law, the colonists did not have the authority to invent laws contrary to English law. Indeed, it was not at all clear what authority they had to pass any laws beyond those for keeping the peace on the island.

Yet they brilliantly conceived an answer to their dilemma by using just that peacekeeping authority. It became the needle's eye through which to pull an entire slave code. They simply assumed that slavery existed (since English law did not mention slavery, colonial legislation could hardly conflict with English law) and then passed laws to deal with disorders expected of slaves. In effect, they reformatted what was a category of labor relations as a subject of criminal law, the latter of which their assembly was legally competent to treat.

Before the century was over the central features of the Barbadian slave code of 1661 (the black code) would reappear in Jamaica and the other English West Indian possessions, as well as South Carolina and Virginia. Black codes would eventually spread throughout the North American colonies. The entire code was not duplicated, nor was it held up as an explicit model, but historians agree that it was influential wherever slaves numbered in excess of 10 percent of the population.

The originality and cogency of the code cannot be denied. Although it had some precedent in earlier legislation on slavery in Barbados, Virginia, and Massachusetts, the Barbados code was unparalleled in scope, coherence, and completeness. The code began by stating that the colony could not exist without slavery, and that so many slaves (by then outnumbering the whites nearly two to one) constituted an inherent problem in terms of public order. In effect, the code was based on what today would be called a policy orientation that put "law and order" above all other concerns. This was something of a fiction, for when the code was promulgated, there had been no slave rebellion and relatively little slave crime (compared, say, to criminal activity in the slums of seventeenth-century London). In fact, the preamble responded to the anxiety and expectations of the master class. They anticipated that slaves would commit crimes and plot rebellion. Thus, from the outset, the code was directed not to the slaves but to the masters, telling them what they must do to ferret out slave crimes and uncover slave plots. The code reminded them that they were not to fraternize with the slaves, and that the boundary between free and slave had to be policed in the most rigorous fashion if the masters were to be safe.

The code defined slaves as chattel property. Slaves could be bought and sold, inherited, and used as liens against property (to secure mortgages or loans) without consulting the will of the slave. Slaves were commodities on the market. Without these provisions, trade in slaves would falter and the commercial viability of the plantations would suffer. But this definition made no sense when applied to criminal law, for the basic assumption of all criminal justice was that the perpetrator of a crime had to act voluntarily. Without mens rea, the capacity to formulate criminal intent, there was no capability. Chattel had no will in the law and was not punished for crimes.

Weapons used in a crime were not found "guilty" and punished. Since the men who enacted the black code knew that slaves were persons with wills of their own, the code simply accepted its own inherent contradiction. Slaves would be bought and sold as though they were chattel but punished for crimes as people. The code provisions on slave crimes assumed that slaves had the requisite moral capacity to know right from wrong and consequently the ability to control their actions.

The code set a very high threshold for liability in white on black crimes. Since one did not destroy the value of one's property, the law assumed that masters would not voluntarily maim or kill their slaves. To be sure, such an assumption ran in the face of human nature; masters and their agents were certainly subject to anger, lust, and madness. They could and did beat, rape, and murder slaves, but the law presumed that they would not and posted no penalties except for the most extreme act. For example, if the master injured or killed a slave in the course of "correction," there was no penalty. Any free white person could kill a slave who assaulted him or her without fear of prosecution. In fact, any free person could strike any slave (not just their own) who was committing a crime, making verbal or physical threats, or neglecting their duties without the master's permission.

Although the Barbados code defined a wide array of slaves' legal misconduct, neither it nor its mainland colonial offshoots in later years penetrated very far into the relations between master and slave on the plantation. To inquire too closely into the way masters punished their own slaves would be to make slavery a public institution. This would have undermined another basic premise of slavery: the slave was the private property of the master. All slave law attempted to strike a balance between the latter fundamental precept and the need to keep order. Thus, the actual number of slave crimes — most of which were undoubtedly committed by slaves against other slaves — not only went unrecorded in the colonial records, they went without official punishment.

The black code did nibble away at the absolute authority of the master. For example, it prescribed punishment for slaves engaging in a number of acts even if these activities were condoned by individual masters. The forbidden activities included congregating without white supervision, leaving the plantation or wandering about the city without a pass, administering medicine without the express permission of the master, carrying a weapon, and (later) engaging in market activities like selling food. All of these practices potentially involved people — guests or visitors, whites from other plantations, consumers of slaves' products — who did not live on the plantation. Nevertheless, masters often ignored these provisions of the code — for example, by allowing slaves to practice folk medicine without supervision, hunt for themselves or for the master's family, sell their own garden produce in town, or visit slave relatives without obtaining a pass for each trip.

The black code denied slaves accused of crimes the rudiments of criminal due process. Along with the protection against self-incrimination, due process as spelled out in federal and state statutes and constitutions includes the right to a public and speedy trial, the right to confront one's accusers, the right to counsel of one's own choosing, and the right to a jury trial "of one's peers." Slaves had none of these rights. They were tried in a speedy fashion and the trial was often well attended, but the purpose of speed and publicity was not to prevent unjust incarceration. Indeed, colonial criminal law did not generally provide jail terms for convicted felons. Instead, trials were swift so that punishment could be equally swift. When a master spoke for a slave in court, the law was conferring a privilege upon the master rather than a right upon the slave. Thus, the 1705 Virginia slave code required the master to appear on behalf of the slave so that no master could complain that his property rights had been ignored when a slave was condemned. Some masters sent lawyers to protect the investment the master had in a particular slave accused of theft, assault, or manslaughter (killing without prior intention) upon another slave. Only rarely did masters provide a defense for slaves accused of murdering a white.

Slaves could not "put themselves upon the country," that is, obtain a jury trial. This was a bedrock of English criminal procedure and it was part of all colonial criminal laws. Instead of jury trials, the Barbados code established "freeholders' courts" composed of a fixed number of justices of the peace (usually two or three) and a greater number of planters sitting as judges. These were widely adopted in other colonies. To be sure, jury trial in criminal cases did not always favor the defendant, and members of juries were not screened (as they are today) to uncover bias, personal interest in the outcome of the case, or prior acquaintance with the parties. What is more, the absence of a jury at a criminal trial was not unusual in the colonies. Faced with paying for a jury in their own cases, most white defendants preferred to "put themselves upon the court" and allow a judge or bench of judges to weigh the facts of their case. Ordinarily this was the prelude to some kind of plea bargain, but slaves lacked the capacity to bargain with the court. In another of the catch-22 situations that marked colonial law, the slave who needed the court to accept his plea could not bargain for it because he was forbidden to address the court.

Moreover, the very reason why courts were willing to accept plea bargains from free defendants worked against offering plea bargains to slaves. White defendants were part of the same society as the judges and jurors. In a criminal justice system without police forces, the courts became the only guarantors of public order. So long as the defendant was willing to bow to the authority of the court, the court was usually willing to offer a lesser sentence. A plea bargain saved the court's time and energy and still maintained its authority. The defendant would pay his fine or do his time in jail and return to society. If he committed a second offense, he would lose his freedom or his life. That prospect presumably would deter him from recidivism.

The court did not have the same power over the slave because the slave had already lost his freedom. The purpose of slave trials was not to return the repentant slave to society but to ensure that other slaves did not commit the same offense. Thus, the court's need to assert its authority made it averse to plea-bargaining with slaves. The only occasions when courts agreed to mitigate sentences for slaves occurred when their masters intervened in their defense or the slave offered to testify against other slaves. In the words of a 1748 Virginia statute, when the slave was suspected of "conspiracy, insurrection, or rebellion," courts were not to show mercy.

In English and colonial law, serious crimes were punishable by death. Slaves suffered the same penalties as other defendants for capital offenses like burglary, robbery, murder, rape, and treason. The slave codes departed in one significant way from conventional sentencing and punishment for serious crimes, however. The manner of punishment of slaves was left to the discretion of the court and might include dismemberment, torture, and burning, whereas the conventional punishment for felony in England was hanging. The purpose of this deviation from English precedent was obvious. For example, in colonial South Carolina the law gave to the freeholders' courts assembled to hear and determine slave felonies the discretion to choose the means of punishment "to deter others [slaves] from offending in the like kind."

In fact, in colonies with many slaves severe punishment appeared to masters to be the only way to protect themselves. Criminal law was the master class's tool. Thus, in the first case recorded in Virginia (1729) in which a jury convicted an overseer for the murder of a slave, the colonial governor commuted the death sentence, reasoning that "executing him for this offense may make the slaves very insolent, and give them occasion to contemn their masters and overseers, which may be of dangerous consequences in a country where the Negroes are so numerous and make the most valuable part of the people's estates." For a similar reason the bodies of slaves convicted and executed for crimes were allowed to hang in public until they rotted, or pieces of the body were impaled on stakes and displayed, for the express purpose of making all slaves stand in fear of the power of their masters' government. Visibility was all-important: on one occasion the chimney of a colonial Virginia courthouse served as the display case for the severed heads of four slaves convicted of plotting the murder of their master.

———

Behind the gory display of body parts lay the masters' pervasive fear of slave conspiracies. Only by grisly deterrence, the master class reasoned, would slaves be dissuaded from rebelling against their condition. The obsessive concern with conspiracy, a striking feature of the Barbados code, would find its way into the law of almost all the colonies. To be sure, fear of conspiracy was a staple of English legal and political thinking, and suspected conspiracies reached the very top of early modern English society and government. Some were frighteningly real, like a plot to blow up the houses of Parliament when James I convened the legislators in 1605. But the criminal law in England did not revolve around the concept of conspiracy. Conspiracy became the axle around which the whole of slave criminal law turned. Indeed one could say that conspiracy was the centerpiece of the slave criminal law. Masters assumed that slaves were by nature disobedient and prone to crime, and they were able to conceal these crimes from their masters precisely because so much of what went on in the slave's quarters was hidden from the master's purview. The masters' conviction that slaves concealed their doings and whispered among themselves led to the fear that slaves were always plotting crimes. Did not slaves routinely steal food and clothing from their masters, break tools, and run away? Any gathering of slaves might also have as its concealed purpose the crime of insurrection. As the Maryland assemblymen concluded in 1717, "It too often happens that Negro slaves and etc. commit many heinous and capital crimes, which are endeavored to be smothered and concealed." Governor Robert Hunter of New York opined in 1713 that "that sort of men" were prone to crime.

Conspiracy was an old category of English criminal law to which slavery gave new urgency and scope. A criminal conspiracy was any meeting of two or more persons to discuss or plan a crime. Conspiracy was also any combination (group, agreement, plan, discussion) that had as its purpose the commission of a crime. The crime need not occur. Conspiracy was considered a separate offense. Thus, conspiracy was far-ranging and could encompass any number of lawful acts that became criminal when a crime ensued. Conspiracy was a perfect way for a government to control various suspect groups. Slaves fit this description, for they were always suspected of plotting to free themselves.

But conspiracy was not a significant infraction in English law. The original definition of the offense, dating from 1304, was a combination or discussion among men whose purpose was to bring a false prosecution in law. In 1591 one of the king's courts excoriated the "wicked sort of men" who plotted to debase the king's justice through perjury. Few cases were recorded under this rubric, the leading one involving a conspiracy to bring a false prosecution in 1611. In it, the Star Chamber, a special royal court that heard cases touching the king's law or his personal interest, found that the false prosecution need not take place for the offense to occur — the plot was sufficient. English legal commentators and authors of manuals for justices of the peace, the latter the first line of criminal law enforcement officers in England, had little to say about the case or the law until judge William Hawkins's *Treatise of Pleas of the Crown* (1716) noted that no man could serve as a juror or give evidence in a crown court if he had been convicted of conspiracy.

The cases of conspiracy that most concerned the crown grew out of prosecutions for violating the excise laws — in other words, conspiracy was an offense concerning the public treasury rather than private interests. It was not classed with felonies like murder, arson, and robbery. As late as 1765, William Blackstone, the leading English jurist of the day, defined conspiracy as an offense "the object of which is to injure by fraud, falsehood, or perjury." Liability for the crime commenced only if the suspect had mens rea, that is, the intention to commit the crime, and when the agreement was concluded. Mere bystanders and attendees were not liable for what they overheard.

Nor was conspiracy a major concern of the colonial lawmakers before the black codes spread. The Massachusetts Laws and Liberties (1641), the first to mention conspiracy, made "conspiring or attempting insurrection" a crime, lumping conspiracy and attempted offenses together. Both required two witnesses, and the defendants had to be active participants in the plot. Both were offenses against the state rather than against a private person. The New Hampshire laws of 1680 adopted this provision under the rubric of "conspiricie against this province." These laws were not directed at slaves or conspiracies of slaves against their masters but at whites who made trouble for colonial governments.

As the number of slaves grew in the southern colonies, the lawgivers applied the Barbados code's definition of conspiracy to slaves. These were simply gatherings of slaves at which a crime was discussed. No attempt to carry out the deed by any of the slaves was necessary to institute the prosecution. All the slaves present (passive as well as active participants in the conversation) were equally liable under the law. In sum, the colonies entirely transformed the older conception of conspiracy in order to apply it to slaves.

The relationship of slave numbers in the population to the shift in the definition of the crime was obvious. For example, the Maryland colonial law of 1692 mirrored the old English definition of the crime of conspiracy in 1692 (plotting to commit perjury). By the second decade of the eighteenth century Maryland's slave population had doubled from what it had been in 1690. In 1717 Maryland legislators amended the colonial code to adopt the Barbados definition of slave conspiracies. Similar laws were adopted in New York and New Jersey after slave conspiracies were uncovered in the early 1710s. The laws included the provision that whites who conspired with slaves against masters would be subject to the same punishments as the slaves. It was the only occasion under colonial law that whites engaged in conspiracies against private persons were not charged with the lesser offense of "attempt." A conspiracy of slaves was an entirely different offense from a conspiracy of free persons to commit perjury or the "attempt" of free persons to commit a crime.

How could the masters prevent offenses they knew would take place but could not uncover? The answer was to prosecute for conspiracy. The prosecution only needed to find a slave or several slaves who could testify that they had overheard other slaves planning a crime or were present when a group of slaves mentioned a crime. No proof was necessary that the crime ever took place or that the slaves made any attempt to further its commission. Conspiracy prosecutions turned crimes merely imagined or anticipated by the master class into opportunities to punish those slaves who dared to speak aloud of resistance to slavery. Thus, as early as 1680 the Virginia colony laws made meetings of slaves without the consent of the master an offense, for gatherings might have "dangerous consequences." In 1708 the New York colonial legislature specifically warned against "slave conspiracy" in a portion of its black code. New Jersey and other colonies followed suit.

Distinguishing the real plots from the merely rumored ones remained a problem. Rumors of slave rebellions were a staple of the oral culture in slave-holding societies. Anxious masters were quick to blame "Negroe plots" on free blacks, new imports, and uppity slaves. One such rumored plot in South Carolina grew out of disgruntled female slaves' anger at male slaves on the same plantation. Unscrupulous magistrates could "plant" a conspiracy by convincing a willing slave to lie about other slaves' words. In this way unruly slaves could be prosecuted even when no proof existed of their misdeeds.

Even courts that were wary of such rumors still had to separate gossip from fact in the testimony of slaves against one another. The law of evidence as it is understood today is one of the most complex and technical areas of study. Even experts cannot agree upon a model code of evidence. Evidence can be declared inadmissible in court for a wide variety of reasons, including (with many qualifications) "hearsay" (secondhand testimony), prejudicial remarks, and overly graphic physical evidence. None of these rules existed in the late seventeenth and early eighteenth centuries. Then, as the English historian James Cockburn has remarked, a trial was an argument between defendant and accuser. Anything might be alleged, and the judges or the jury in jury trials had to use their common sense to screen out the more illogical assertions.

In most slave trials, the problem of weighing evidence was even more complicated, for slaves were not tried by juries, nor did they have the right to argue with their accusers, call witnesses in their own defense, or testify on their own behalf. Slave witnesses desired to please the judges. They brought along a raft of personal grudges and attachments and represented a foreign culture with different ways of seeing, hearing, and telling stories. The judges had to make sense of all this information according to their own standards of probity, which might be entirely different from that of the slaves.

Because of the perceived unreliability of slave testimony, slaves were not allowed to testify against nonslaves, and even in cases involving only slaves the defendant or slave witness was only allowed to answer those questions directly put to him. In the 1710s some colonies shifted their stance on slave testimony, permitting slaves to testify against other slaves. Only in this way could conspiracies be revealed. Maryland (1717), South Carolina (1723), Virginia (1723), and North Carolina (1741) allowed slaves to testify against other slaves without swearing to tell the truth under oath. The rationale, repeated in all the colonies' black codes, was that conspiracies by slaves were "known only" to other slaves. Not admitting the testimony of slave witnesses to a conspiracy would allow the conspiracy to remain hidden until it bore fruit. As the New York law of 1730 put it, slaves could only testify against other slaves in cases of "plotting or confederacy amongst themselves, either to run away, kill, or destroy their master, mistress, or any other person, or burning of houses, barns, or stacks of hay or of corne." Colonial law stated that the evidence of one slave was sufficient to convict, which was a departure from English rules requiring the testimony of two witnesses, or one with "pregnant circumstances," in capital cases.

Two dilemmas arose as a result of this solution to the problem of getting and assessing evidence in suspected slave conspiracies: how to prevent slaves from falsely accusing other slaves of planning crimes, and how to stop masters from hiding slaves suspected of crimes from justice. Ordinarily the law ensured the reliability of testimony during a trial by requiring parties to testify under oath. This assumed that the witnesses were Christians. Oaths subjected a lying witness to the judgment of heaven, a far more terrifying prospect than prosecution for perjury. But in most cases, slaves were not Christians and could not take an oath even if allowed to do so. The second dilemma was evidently widespread enough to concern the lawmakers. Masters not only refused to bring slaves accused of crimes to court but hid accused slaves or even transported them out of the colony. To resolve the first quandary the colonies passed statutes ordering that slaves who perjured themselves were to have their ears nailed to the pillory and then cut off, after the slave had received thirty-nine lashes on their backs "well laid on." The second obstacle was overcome by dipping into the public treasury to recompense masters for slaves executed or exiled for crimes.

The best way to penetrate slave conspiracies was to gain confessions from slave conspirators. Slave criminal law welcomed confessions, but few slaves confessed to crimes. Thomas D. Morris, a leading scholar of colonial slave law, found fifteen confessions throughout the eighteenth century in the eleven Virginia counties he examined. This is not a large number compared to the number of slaves brought to court. Slaves might have confessed crimes to their owners and been punished without any record of the crime. If a crime did not come to court, it was not recorded. Mentions of such cases in a few planters' diaries and overseers' journals from the colonial and antebellum periods suggest that confession and punishment out of court was much more common than official proceedings initiated by masters against slaves, if only because masters did not want to lose valuable slaves.

Even those confessions of conspiratorial complicity that occurred were likely to be involuntary. An involuntary confession cannot be trusted, as the U.S. Supreme Court reminded law-enforcement officials in *Miranda v. Arizona* (1966). Some slave confessions in cases of alleged conspiracy were made in the hope of a reduced sentence or leniency from the court. More were induced by torture or the fear of physical harm. Against a confession coerced by the authorities slaves had little remedy. They could recant or become silent, but these were not effective strategies to avert punishment. Instead, by listening to what the court wanted them to say about supposed co-conspirators, they learned how to inform on others. The latter may have been part of a plot, merely bystanders, or even slaves that had had no hand in the affair but that the accused disliked.

English and English colonial courts rarely ordered the torture of any suspect (except for treason cases), but there is evidence that in cases involving slave insurrections, captured rebels were routinely tortured to obtain the identities of other rebels. One would never think to torture one's chattel, but this final irony in slave criminal law did not seem to bother the courts. So terrifying was the prospect of a widespread conspiracy that colonial officials did not hesitate to order the torture of slave suspects.

———

Might not the colonial authorities have taken a different path? If the danger of slave uprising so affrighted them, why did the law-givers not make slavery less oppressive? A tantalizing possibility suggests itself here: Had the Barbadian code not been available as a model, might not the other English have adopted a more humane and flexible system of slave law? In frontier societies with a small number of slaves — for example, the first years of the South Carolina colony, in Dutch New Netherland before 1664 (when the English arrived and gained control of the colony), and in much of northern New England — the lot of slaves was, in practice, far better than under the Barbados code. The correlative of leniency in the law seems to have been the small percentage of slaves in the total population and the diminished value of their labor.

Take the case of the New Netherland slave law. Although the home government was well aware that Dutch merchants transported slaves in their ships and sold them, and that the Dutch masters of plantations in Brazil and the West Indies used slaves, it did not much concern itself with slavery. It issued no general rulings on the subject to the companies chartered in the Netherlands. Nor were there any major court opinions on slavery in the home provinces. In Dutch Brazil and Surinam, where slaves were numerous, the law was harsh. In New Netherland, where slaves were few, the law was lenient. True, slaves had to work on public projects or their masters would be fined; slaves could not assemble, dance, or play musical instruments without permission; slaves could not travel without passes, gamble with whites, or buy firearms from them; and slaves could not carry on businesses of their own. Slaves' behavior was to be closely monitored; in particular, slave feasts and other celebrations were curbed. But overall the Dutch authorities were lax in their regulation of slavery. There was no prohibition against masters educating their slaves, and some acted as clerks in their masters' businesses. The law encouraged slaves to attend worship services and facilitated religious instruction of slaves. Even while in bondage, slaves could testify in the New Netherland courts. The law also enjoined masters to care for their slaves. Indeed, the Dutch seem to have had little aversion to allowing masters to free slaves. Free persons of color could own property (including slaves) and could serve in the militia.

Even though the Dutch regarded Africans as inferior — free Africans were always at risk of being denounced as runaway slaves — the Dutch nevertheless introduced the "half-freedom" concept. According to it, slaves who had served well would agree to perform public works and pay an annual fee to the company in return for considerable freedom of movement and the right to hire themselves out to employers ("self-hires"). The Dutch West India Company (owner of the largest number of slaves) benefited, for it had little for the slaves to do much of the year and was relieved of the expense of caring for its bondsmen. The half-free could and did petition for freedom for their children. There was thus little evidence of the kind of brutality that characterized slavery in the Caribbean.

Why the leniency? The rulers of New Netherland were in no need of slaves as plantation laborers because the colony was a trading post rather than an agricultural venture. To perform heavy labor in the city of New Amsterdam, the company encouraged the importation of slaves, with all but a few coming from the other colonies (principally Curaçao). However, the cost of slaves was so great, and the growing season in New Netherland so short in comparison with that in the West Indies, slaves were simply not very profitable to masters in the northern Dutch colony. Nor did the Dutch merchants profit from the slave trade to the city of New Amsterdam. The Caribbean market was far more lucrative. The same economic considerations that led to the rigors of the Barbadian black code fostered the leniency of the Dutch slave regime in New Netherland.

Governed by the same harsh logic, the English law of slavery in the colony of New York after 1664 was far harsher than Dutch law in New Netherland. The English in New York had an economic interest in promoting slavery in the colony that the Dutch did not. The ruler of the colony was James Stuart, duke of York and younger brother of King Charles II. James was the director and chief financial beneficiary of the Royal African Company, which had a monopoly on the English overseas slave trade. The overseas trading merchants of New York City (the new name for New Amsterdam) would participate in the trade along with English merchants. They had every reason to fashion a harsh slave code.

All of this related to the connection between the city and the English sugar islands. The city would become one of the chief ports of departure for the carrying trade in foodstuffs to Barbados, Jamaica, and other English West Indian colonies. In return, New York City received slaves from the West Indies. Even after the royal company's monopoly ended, New York City merchants would retain almost as strong a stake in the economic success of the sugar islands as the planters themselves — and that success depended on slave labor at both ends. There was thus every incentive for the English in the colony to adopt the strictest rules for governing slaves. The answer to the hypothetical question is clear: had there been no Barbadian slave code as a model, New York and the other colonies with an economic interest in slavery would have passed laws very similar to those written in Barbados.

Crucial provisions of the New York slave code followed the pattern introduced in Barbados and copied in the South. The colonial legislature introduced major slave legislation in 1702, 1708, 1712, 1730, and 1731. Each enactment repeated the provisions of its predecessor and added further restrictions on the activities of slaves. The 1702 law made it lawful for masters to correct or punish slaves for misconduct, the latter defined by the master. This gave to masters complete discretion in the manner of their "correction," although they were still held accountable for wounding and killing slaves without cause. The law also forbade the gathering of more than three slaves without the master's consent or presence. Finally, to prevent slaves from competing in the marketplace against free persons, the law barred slaves from buying and selling in the streets without the master's permission. All of these provisions reversed the relative leniency of the earlier Dutch law and undermined slaves' attempts to better themselves economically. In 1708 a statute made it a felony for slaves to conspire to commit murder. In effect, any slave who discussed such an act was subject to the severest penalty.

The law of 1712 regulated manumission by requiring masters wishing to free a slave to post a bond of two hundred pounds (known as colony money) guaranteeing the slave's good behavior. The new law also made it a crime for anyone to harbor runaways. An arson and murder plot hatched by two dozen newly arrived slaves had prompted the new law. To deal with future conspiracies, the statute of 1712 imported the freeholders' courts introduced in Barbados. Two justices of the peace and five white property holders named by the governor could hear and determine a case of crime alleged against a slave. The slave could be brought before this court on a warrant based on the information of a free person. No grand jury indictment was necessary and no jury would be empaneled to determine facts. As in Barbados and other colonies, there was no appeal from the judgment of the freeholders' court and punishment for a felony (a capital offense) might be anything that the court decreed.

In 1730 New York lawgivers made it a crime for anyone to "entertain slaves" without their masters' consent, a law directed at the innkeepers and tavern owners who allowed slaves to drink and gamble during the evening hours. Darkness seemed to be the ally of the slave who wished to conceal his movements, or so the lawgivers presumed. In 1731 a new statute required that any slave out after dark must carry a lantern. Meetings of more than three slaves after dark were barred. For the lawgivers, concealment, conspiracy, and crime walked hand in hand at night — and in some cases they were right. In all of these laws, the authorities plainly feared slave conspiracies and made the prevention of conspiracy the focus of the criminal law for slaves.

The English colonial law of slavery was the outgrowth of economic desire of a handful of free men, but it affected all people. By making laws that presumed slaves conspired against their masters and against the state, the colony built a wall of suspicion and hatred between the races. By asking, as the law did, that all whites police the boundary between free and slave, and by making it so difficult to cross for slaves to become free, the law made freedom and slavery into fixed categories that defined the very nature of society.

CHAPTER 2

A Tale of Two Cities

The free and the slave lived in close proximity in New York City. Most slaves inhabited the same dwellings as their masters or resided in nearby rentals. It was a face-to-face society, for the average master owned only one or two slaves and most worked as domestic help or in neighborhood workshops. Even slaves rented out to others by their masters or allowed to sell their own labor — for example, on the docks — walked the streets next to whites. Slaves in New York City were part of the everyday experiences of whites and vice versa. Neither group had any illusions about the other, and whatever emotional involvements there might be — whether anger, envy, fear, fellowship, or admiration — were hard to hide.

It was the physical structure of the colonial city that dictated these domestic arrangements. The cities of the British North American colonies contained a mere 1 percent of the colonial population, but because no city was larger than two square miles in size, the cities were the most densely populated of all colonial living sites. Indeed, colonial cities teemed with people. In 1760 Philadelphia boasted twenty-five thousand people in its 1 square mile of settled area, while in 1771 New York City packed nearly twenty thousand people into its 1.1 square miles of land. People lived close to their work, preferring to rent subdivided lots rather than move to undeveloped or vacant lands, and urban builders preferred sites close to waterfronts.

Cities were economic hubs, marketplaces, busy manufacturing centers, and conspicuous meeting points of the empire and its far-flung provinces. Indeed, imperial officials and representatives of local governments often met in different rooms within the same buildings. In the city, government and commerce joined hands. Colonial newspapers published reports from Britain and advertised shipments of goods from all around the Atlantic rim.

Cities were exciting, noisy, smelly, and dangerous places to live. Traffic was a nightmare. Runaway horses and wagons trampled the unwary pedestrian. Carters and wagon drivers were notorious for their foul mouths and sometimes raced each other up and down crowded thoroughfares. Parking rules did not exist. The noise level of traffic kept residents awake well into the night since the wheels of wagons bringing farmers' goods to market were ironclad and howled like banshees.

A few cities had been planned to provide easy traffic flow. Annapolis, the capital of Maryland, looked like a wheel, with the government buildings forming the axle. Philadelphia exhibited a giant gridlike pattern. But other cities, like New York and Boston, had no master plan and grew haphazardly. Boston resembled an overgrown New England village, with narrow, winding streets and an open pasture in the center of town. New York's streets were laid out at jagged angles and were bisected by a canal that for much of the seventeenth century was little more than an open sewer.

The upper and lower classes mingled freely on the streets, which exhibited striking juxtapositions of great wealth and wrenching poverty. Cheek by jowl with the merchants' elegant and spacious town houses stood the rickety hovels of sailors and the three-story wooden walk-ups of laborers. No one passing through the city could miss seeing the extremes of the human condition. City leaders assayed a variety of strategies to deal with the poor. "Home relief" for the "worthy poor," who were too old or infirm to work, consisted of food and fuel delivered to the home, but most cities refused home relief to its neediest denizens — free blacks and Indians. Some of the cities built workhouses in which the poor lived and worked for their keep, but these soon became overcrowded and resembled prisons more than charitable institutions.

To narrow the gap between rich and poor, city boosters like Philadelphian Benjamin Franklin endeavored to improve everyday life in the city. To upgrade the lot of ordinary people in Philadelphia, he helped establish a Free Library Company in 1731, a public hospital, and elementary schools. In addition, he was an early advocate of street lighting and regular garbage collection. Still, as Franklin grudgingly admitted, all the new cities faced serious problems providing adequate public services. There were no zoning restrictions to control building. Rickety warehouses were everywhere. They were often literally slapped together and sometimes fell apart without warning. All wooden construction also posed fire hazards for which the cities were unprepared. Bucket brigades could not cope with the danger of sprawling expansion, particularly when warehouses contained gunpowder and other explosives.

The threat of fire reminded all concerned that the cities depended on water reserves. The quality of drinking water presented even more problems than the quantity of water available to fight fires. Private wells in New York City were brackish and germ-ridden. The public water supply did not improve until 1753, when a new tax underwrote repairs and increased the number of city water pumps. Underground sewers drained the water, but the smell and the spillover from the sewers made certain street corners noxious. William Livingston, a New York City lawyer, cited one such nuisance as "Rotten Row," where "the putrid stink arising from that sink of corruption" entered the neighborhood shops. Porters — most often slaves — carried human waste out of the cities in tubs since the cities' leaky sewers could not be trusted to do the job. People dumped other refuse, including food slops, into the streets and alleys. Pigs roamed the streets, consuming human waste and depositing their own in its place.

One might have expected, from the close proximity of their persons and the commonalities of their experience of city life, that whites and blacks would have come to an understanding, a kind of grudging mutual respect, if not a sense of equality. Nothing could be further from the truth. The impact of the slave laws was so profound that it divided the city into two. One city was free and white, the other enslaved and black. The white city was a place where a shrewd and able man might make a fortune, live well, and count himself a king in his own country. Even the poor apprentice, the immigrant, and the religious dissenter might share this dream, though few would realize it. Whites were divided along ethnic, religious, and class lines, but the divisions were never so great nor so insurmountable as that between white and black.

The other city was marked not so much by poverty as by the legal infirmities imposed on people of color. Simply because of the perceived darkness of their skin, some men and women could never hope for success or personal independence. Under English rule the slave was likely to remain a slave, knowing that his or her children would fare no better. The dark-skinned Indian and free African American's dreams were also deferred, for they, too, could not rise above their lowly station.

To be sure, there were divisions among people of color. Africans from Senegal and Nigeria spoke languages and had customs different from the Congolese and Angolans. Slaves from the West Indies looked down on the newly imported Africans, while native-born slaves (African Americans) and free persons of color regarded themselves as higher in status than the newcomers. Yet all shared the burdens that the law imposed on people of color. In later years an antebellum southern defender of slavery would insist that no progressive society could be without its "mudsill" on which the better classes wiped their feet. The people of color in New York City were its mudsill, and their city was different from that of their masters.

By suggesting that slave law and its repercussions divided the city in two, I do not mean to suggest that whites were not divided along ethnic and class lines. The sharp divisions between rich and poor were everywhere evident in the city, for the laborer's hovel stood in the alley behind the rich man's mansion. The poor man could not hide his desperate straits and the rich man flaunted his wealth. Ethnic divisions were a bit more subtle but just as deep. The Dutch elite accepted English political supremacy and made marriage and partisan alliances with the English ruling classes, but the ordinary Dutch resisted Anglicization. German newcomers to the colony resented the condescension with which the Anglo-colonial upper classes greeted all foreigners. Scottish, Scots-Irish (northern Ireland Protestants), and Irish immigrants were equally unhappy with the attitude of the English governing elite.

What held these ill-tempered groups together was their share in the economic benefits of slavery. The Dutch and English elites formed companies to replace the defunct Royal African Company's slave trade. Leading Dutch and English merchants, who were joined by French Huguenot and Scottish emigré entrepreneurs, brought slaves into the colony and shipped foodstuffs, clothing, and fuel to the West Indies. Scots-Irish, Germans, and Dutch farmers in rural areas around the city produced the grain and livestock which fed the sugar islands. More than half of the Middle Atlantic region's trade was with the West Indies. The profits of the trade were reinvested in the region's domestic (internal) economy. The overseas merchants built warehouses and wharfs, as well as city mansions and country estates. The wealth trickled down to the urban working poor and out to the farmsteads. The swelling commercial activity attracted immigrants whose cheap labor fostered further growth of the economy. From 1700 to 1760 the whole colony's population rose from 19,000 to 117,100. The slave portion of this increase — from 3,700 in 1700 to 29,000 in 1760 — was an indispensable accommodation to the city economy.

There were political partisanships among the whites. The first English immigrants were divided in their political loyalties. The English who settled Long Island were Puritans and preferred a political tie to Connecticut. Other English settlers owed their position and power to the ruler of the colony, James Stuart. Even after he was driven from the throne in 1688, they remained loyal to him. Another faction in the colony saw the Jacobites as closet Roman Catholics and determined to root them out. These divisions opened the door to violent factionalism in New York City politics. In 1689 Dutch inhabitants of the colony who had never reconciled themselves to English rule joined with the virulent anti-Catholic partisans to establish a temporary government under the leadership of a German-born merchant named Jacob Leisler. In 1691 Leisler was hanged for refusing to relinquish power to William and Mary's appointed governor. His obstinance was symbolic of a deep gulf between the well-to-do, who supported the new monarchs, and the poorer classes, who longed for a kind of independence from aristocratic rule.

New York City was a locus for these plots among whites, for it was the focal point, the raison d'être, of the colony. The city governed itself according to a charter (a grant of privileges) from the crown. Unlike modern cities, it was not an agency of the state. Its officers consisted of a mayor and aldermen sitting in the common council. Under the charter of 1730, the corporation of the city of New York owned City Hall and all other municipal buildings, all the waste or common land, and much of the waterfront. It could not tax the city's inhabitants, but it could regulate a wide range of their activities, including what they charged for food and labor. The voters in the city consisted of its "freemen," and these, according to Edwin Burrows and Michael Wallace, constituted a third of the entire adult population of the city. But the shopkeepers and craftsmen who made up the bulk of this voting force cared little about government, so by default an aristocracy of the counting house and the manor house governed the city.

The next rung up the political ladder was the colonial government. Powerful mercantile families in the city joined with equally powerful landholding families up the Hudson River to divide colonial offices. All adult white males with a freehold worth at least forty pounds, as well as all tenants with lifetime leases and all freemen in the cities of Albany and New York, could vote. Although the franchise in the colony was remarkably broad when compared to the voters in England, the voters in the colony generally deferred to their betters when it came to polls. (Voting was not secret, and voters thus had to be careful not to offend powerful candidates.) Such political deference was not social — lower-class men and women often resented the posing of their superiors — but economic. The wealthy underwrote the debts and secured the liabilities of the poor. This was the reward for deference. The poor expected and the rich often provided charity, bonds for good behavior, and patronage.

Historians still disagree as to how aristocratic the rulers of the colony actually were. Theirs was not a hereditary aristocracy, although some had come from noble families in Europe. Instead, the magnates of colonial politics were well-to-do members of families that had gained power in the late seventeenth century. These included Dutch, English, and Huguenot clans like the Philipses, Livingstons, and the DeLanceys. In addition, those families that had dominated the New Netherland colony — like the Van Dams, Van Courtlandts and Van Rensselaers — retained their offices and wealth in the English colony through shrewd alliances with the leading English families. Though conservative in their political views, the members of this colonial aristocracy had no overriding political ideology. Factions and alliances were personal rather than ideological, and such alliances as did appear in the lower house constantly shifted.

The focal point of this political flux at the upper echelons of the colony was the governor's office. Governors were chosen in England and sent to the colony. In theory the governorship was a very lucrative post for which politicians in England jockeyed and which the secretary of state for the Southern Department — for much of this period the politically astute duke of Newcastle — handed out to men with powerful backing in the home country. The post was worth at least ten thousand pounds a year, but collecting the salary from the colonial legislature was not easy. The fees from office, the rents on lands, and the payments for grants were as uncertain as the salary. Factions based on personal allegiance, party alliance, and plain old corruption had made New York politics raucous for the first third of the eighteenth century. So virulent were the outspoken enemies of one governor that they announced he paraded about the mansion in women's clothing (a charge he denied).

The job of governor would have taxed a saint and exhausted a marathoner. He was the commander in chief of the colonial armed forces, though the militia was inept and the royal forces stationed in the colony paid little heed to the governor or his lieutenant. He was the head of the chancery court, though none of the governors had any legal experience. He was the man who appointed the colonial councillors (the upper legislative chamber) over which he presided, though they often turned on him and refused to support his policies.

Still, his power on paper was immense. The governor named the justices of the supreme court and the judges of lower courts (according to instructions he brought with him from England), as well as all manner of other royal officials, down to the men who went looking for tall pine trees for the royal navy's masts. He had the power to order the assembly into session, to call for new elections, and to set its agenda, but the assembly could diddle with and delay his salary, which gave them a counterbalancing power over him.

By the 1720s two powerful sets of coalitions had emerged in colonial government that would persist into the 1770s. One, allied with Governor William Burnet, included the Philipse and DeLancey families, merchants with close ties to the imperial authorities. Lawyers like Richard Bradley, John Chambers, and James Murray would join this faction and be rewarded with posts on the governor's council and other offices. The opposition rallied around Lewis Morris, a land speculator and lawyer who sat on the council and was chief justice of the Supreme Court. Behind Morris stood the Livingston family, Dutch clans like the Van Dams, and city lawyers like James Alexander and William Smith.

Today one might not think a handful of lawyers on either side of an issue would carry much weight, but then there were relatively few lawyers in the colony, and they had exclusive access to the lucrative mayor's court in the city and the supreme court. Men like Smith and Alexander were also the closest thing to a law school in the colony. Young men who wanted to practice law and could not get to England for training "read" law in Smith's and Alexander's offices. When they were ready, the two senior lawyers sponsored their students' entry to the bar and provided referrals.

These factions attacked one another with a vengeance during the tenure of Governor William Cosby (1732–1736). Some governors were highly conscientious, while others were simply caterpillars of corruption, but all of them saw the post as a way to extract wealth from the colony. The worst of these was Cosby. He came from a large family and made his way up the ladder in the army. He married well and in 1718 became governor of the Atlantic island colony of Minorca. There he established a reputation for ruthlessness and avarice. In 1732 his patrons in England secured him the governorship of New York. He demanded the portion of his salary for the period of time before he actually arrived, as well as control of western lands, which the assembly — led by the powerful forces of Rip Van Dam, the Livinsgton family, and Lewis Morris — resisted. Cosby replaced Morris with James DeLancey as chief justice and then created a new court of exchequer for the express purpose of filing a suit to gain his back pay. DeLancey had legal training at the Inns of Court (a kind of law school) in London but lacked practical experience as a judge or a lawyer. While Cosby plotted to extract every shilling he could from his post, the colony stumbled from one political controversy to another.

When the anti-Cosby forces turned to John Peter Zenger's *New York Weekly Journal* to promote their cause, Cosby ordered the paper shut down and the editor tried for seditious libel. Under the English law of seditious libel, which made criticism of the government a criminal offense, all Attorney General Richard Bradley had to prove was that Zenger had printed the attack against Cosby. The case came to trial in April 1735. When Zenger's lawyers James Alexander and William Smith objected to the presence of DeLancey as chief justice (he being an interested party), DeLancey removed them from the case and denied them the right to practice before the Supreme Court. Of the two remaining stalwarts of the bar, James Murray was in the governor's pocket, which left John Chambers — already appointed recorder (and hence council member) by the governor — as the only man who could defend Zenger. Merely a competent pleader, Chambers promised to do his best, but the Morris faction secretly turned to Philadelphia lawyer Andrew Hamilton (no relation to revolutionary leader Alexander Hamilton), who convinced the jury that they could acquit Zenger if they believed his publications were true. It was a sleight-of-hand worthy of a Cicero, for the law was on the side of the prosecution, but the jury bought the argument and acquitted Zenger. A year later, in 1736, his avarice still unslaked, Cosby died of complications resulting from tuberculosis.

Reverberations from Cosby's tenure continued to roil the surface of colonial politics. Van Dam assumed that he would become acting governor, but the crown named George Clarke, a longtime placeman in the colony (he had arrived in 1707 and had occupied a variety of posts under a succession of governors, the last being Cosby), as its lieutenant governor. He was supported by the Philipse and DeLancey families — who, like Clarke himself, had served Cosby — as well as by officials like Bradley. Clarke repaid their loyalty by retaining them in office.

Horsmanden, another Cosby loyalist, was made the recorder of the city, a judge of various courts (in the colonies there was no prohibition against holding multiple offices), and a member of the council for the colony. William Smith Jr., who wrote a history of the colony in the 1750s, regarded Horsmanden as nothing more than a sycophant, but the recorder's office — which influenced the running of the mayor's court and controlled entry to the legal profession — was a key legal post. Clarke may not have cared whether Horsmanden was up to the job. Loyalty mattered more than skill. The lieutenant governor even made his son, William Jr., a member of the council. Under Clarke and with his full support James DeLancey retained the chief justiceship. The Morris faction opposed Clarke, but could not dislodge him.

Clarke, for so long an aloof and distant figure in New York politics, had no knack for politicking and no following in the colony save what his office and his patrons in England gained him. Indeed, whatever party he backed was sure to lose favor with the voters. He had to dissolve the old assembly because it was full of Morrisites, but its successor, elected in 1737, was even more opposed to Clarke. In particular, New York City returned a full slate of Morris followers. Clarke knew he had to make some concessions and reluctantly reached a compromise with the leaders of the new assembly. He could not, however, win the favor of the city, for when he swung to the Morris side, its electors turned around and chose men from the Philipse-DeLancey bloc. Clarke staggered along until 1743, when he was replaced by George Clinton.

Given the politicization of the legislature and the executive branches of the colonial government, it should come as no surprise that colonial judicial posts were political plums. On the lowest rung of the judicial system stood the courts that justices of the peace held to hear misdemeanor cases and settle minor property, contract, and labor disputes. The justices' courts also had some administrative and regulatory duties. One of these sat in each county; thus New York City (New York County) had one. Although William Smith Jr., a lawyer himself, thought the justices on the bench of the county courts were poorly trained (he complained that some could "neither write nor read"), the justices had great discretion and were often local political bigwigs.

Alongside the justices' courts was the mayor's court, a survival from the seventeenth century, modeled upon the courts in Europe that adjudicated disputes among merchants. London had such a court, as did Amsterdam and New Amsterdam. In the 1730s the court still heard cases of contract, debt, labor relations (including the sale of slaves and the treatment of servants), slander, regulation of market practices, pricing, and traditional litigation over estates, wills, and some minor criminal offenses. The bench of the court included the recorder of the city and its aldermen. The bar was restricted to those men approved by the governor. These included mith, Murray, Alexander, Chambers, and a few others — in effect, as closed a corporation as the city itself. Those lawyers permitted to practice jealously guarded their monopoly. Not until 1745 was every lawyer who practiced before the supreme court of the colony allowed to bring and argue suits in the mayor's court.

Above the justices' courts and the mayor's court was the Court of Common Pleas. On its bench sat three justices appointed by the governor. It met twice a year to hear civil litigation. At the apex of the judicial system was the Supreme Court, whose three judges received a fee of ten shillings for every case they heard and a salary of three hundred pounds a year. Although this court had jurisdiction in all important cases, the judges were often political figures with no particular legal training. An exchequer court, modeled upon the court that decided cases touching the royal treasury, and a court of chancery, likewise modeled upon an English court that delivered a variety of special remedies (such as injunctions) completed the system. The governor (almost always a retired soldier or a veteran politician) was the chancellor, providing a perfect example of a position unfitted for the man who held it and a man invariably unfitted to perform the functions of his job.

Monitoring the operation of the colonial government from afar were the administrators of the empire in England. In law the colony belonged to the crown, but in fact the Hanoverian kings of England paid little attention to the day-to-day governance of their American colonies. King George II relied on his ministers of state, his legal advisers, and the Board of Trade to run the empire. In his name they had the power to approve all colonial laws. His high courts had final jurisdiction in cases appealed from the colony. From England to New York City went a myriad of minor functionaries to collect customs duties, chase smugglers, assist the naval forces gathering for the war against Spain in the Caribbean, and run Fort George in the city. The English army had forces stationed in the colony and the Royal Navy's ships protected the port of New York.

The city, colonial, and imperial political systems overlapped in their duties and powers, but they had a common purpose. The rulers of the city, the colony, and the empire recognized the importance of commerce, land development, and overseas trade. Profits from all of these activities flowed through the city and then out to the many way stations of empire in the Atlantic. Through the portals of the city came the young men who wanted to make their fortunes in America, men on the make like Colden and Horsmanden. Political division, like class and ethnic conflict, faded before the prospect of the tall cargo ships in the harbor, the bustling wharves and warehouses, the rows of elegant merchant establishments, and above all the trade with the West Indies. None of this, it seemed, would have been possible without slavery.

In the meantime, sailors, shipbuilders, and dockworkers had to be entertained, so a spiderweb of taverns, coffee shops, teahouses, and retail outlets spun out over the southern tip of Manhattan island. These establishments sold imported and domestic rum, local beers and ciders, and a wide variety of consumer durables. From towns, villages, and outlying farms came the garden produce of an entire region. Often the food was brought to town by slaves driving farmers' carts. The slaves would sometimes set up their own kiosks to sell the produce or hawk their wares like peddlers through the streets. In the dramshops (the lowliest of the taverns) slaves and free men drank elbow to elbow. Owners ignored the law as long as the slave could pay for his purchase. Who among the whites could imagine the city without slavery?

———

Essential as they might be for the white city to prosper, slaves knew a different city from that of their masters. They traditionally performed tasks no white man would willingly do, such as hauling and dumping trash and excrement, sweeping streets, and slaughtering livestock. In 1664 slaves comprised a fifth of the population, totaling some 375 men and women. The 375 Africans (roughly 75 of whom were free persons) grew to over 3,000 slaves by 1710, with very little increase in the number of free blacks. By 1731 there were almost 1,600 slaves in New York City proper (that is, the tip of the island of Manhattan) and Long Island, and nearly 5,000 in the New York–New Jersey area. By 1731 blacks constituted 18 percent of the total population of the city. In 1738 a rough census counted 8,945 whites and 1,719 blacks residing in New York County, with all but a few of the blacks being slaves. In 1738 Kings County, Long Island, was home to another 600 slaves. More lived in Queens County and \n the island that included Richmond County. A few lived and worked on the manors along the Hudson valley. Many more dwelled across the Hudson River in New Jersey.

Until the middle of the eighteenth century, over two thirds of imported slaves came to New York from the West Indies, a return on the flow of foodstuffs that the New York merchants sent to the West Indian sugar colonies. From 1715 to 1740 some 2,961 slaves arrived from the West Indies, compared to 961 from Africa and 171 from other mainland colonies. The majority of slaves thus came to the city "seasoned" by their stay in the islands, able to speak some English, and practiced in the arts that slaves needed to survive within the system that bound them. But in the period under study that demographic began to change. More and more slaves were imported directly from Africa.

By the end of the 1730s, the increasing number of slaves imported directly from Africa meant that a wide variety of African customs reappeared in the daily lives of New York City slaves. For example, a recently excavated slave burial ground reveals that parents adorned their dead children in African-style shell and bead jewelry. Slave dwelling quarters in Brooklyn were constructed in African fashion, with interior walls facing the door. Pride in the slaves' African heritage also increased with the arrival of newcomers. The influx of slaves from Africa also meant that the bargaining power of individual slaves — for example, to induce a master to purchase a spouse — dwindled. Moreover, the newcomers' African customs conflicted with Christian norms. Early in the century one optimistic cleric reported that "swarms of negroes" had approached him for instruction, but later another complained that "few slaves" attended services. Ministers in the city warned the newcomers against persisting in the practices of polygamy and divination. Even when slaves converted to Christianity, skeptics insisted that the slaves used their new religion as an excuse to avoid work on the sabbath and holidays. Other wary observers worried that the slaves' adoption of Christianity brought them into too close a contact with whites — for example, at Pentecost and Christmas. Despite the need for slave labor and the everyday concourse of black and white workers, whites still resented blacks who crossed the boundary separating the two cities.

Few slaves in the city worked alone or exclusively with other slaves. Unlike the planters in the West Indies and the rice-growing areas of the Carolina coast, most New York City masters owned only a few slaves, employing them close to home. A few masters owned more than a dozen slaves, but these holdings hardly compared to the many hundreds of slaves working the fields on the great plantations to the south. Relatively speaking, the conditions of work for New York City slaves were far easier than in the plantation colonies. To judge from the number of advertisements masters or overseers placed in local newspapers, slaves in New York and New Jersey were less likely to run away than slaves in the Carolinas. Masters knew this, and during conspiracy trials they argued that slaves were pampered in the city. Certainly they had more freedom of movement and contact with whites. One measure of the greater Anglicization of slaves in New York compared to those to the south appears in the advertisements that masters posted for runaways. In South Carolina these advertisement often noted that the slave could not speak English. In New York and New Jersey, the advertisements warned that runaways spoke Dutch and Spanish as well as English, played musical instruments, and plied trades and crafts.

In a number of cases English masters, conceding that slaves had contributed to the success of their businesses and to family life, provided for the slaves' freedom, but the law on manumission tightened in 1712 and remained restrictive throughout the first four decades of the century. Slaves freed after 1712 were not allowed to own their own homes. Whatever the law might say, however, relations between slaves and masters were always a matter of negotiation. Some slaves seem to have been trusted implicitly by their masters, while others complained that they were mistreated regularly.

One common area of negotiation was the independence slaves sought to begin their own families. The sex ratio of slaves in the colony favored men. Masters had to give their male slaves permission to visit with other masters' female slaves. The law did not sanctify slave marriages (to do so would have made it difficult for masters to sell one of the spouses without the other) nor did it require that masters allow slaves to visit spouses on a regular basis. Many slaves either did not marry, engaged in serial relationships without benefit of marriage, or married according to African (serial) rather than colonial (monogamous) customs. Free blacks and Indians could and did marry slaves, but these unions were not easy to maintain. Moreover, married slaves could not protect their spouses against abusive masters or renters. Slave offspring were not governed by parents, for masters had the ultimate say in matters of the domicile and this included the disciplining of slave children. Once again the two cities were closely connected but never fully integrated.

The more slaves the merchants and shippers brought into the city, the more slaves one could find in the streets and workplaces. Observers noted the omnipresence of slaves in public. On holidays and the sabbath, slaves played games, went to services, held parties, and, according to the local court, joined in "disorders and other mischiefs" with white apprentices and servants. Pass as many statutes as the authorities might, there was no way to stop whites and blacks from coming together to drink, gamble, and commit crimes. The harsher the laws became, the more alienated the slaves appeared. The more the authorities warned against slave conspiracies, the wider the gulf separating the two cities grew.

Thus, when slaves were suspected of committing serious crimes, the hue and cry was especially shrill. A 1708 case of robbery-murder committed by two slaves against their master's family petrified the entire colony. The slave felons were depicted as "most barbarous" and the punishments were especially gruesome. The two convicts were burned to death for "petty treason."

A slave rebellion on April 1, 1712, supported the whites' vision of some slaves as "hellish." Twenty-four slaves participated, all of them Coromantees from what was then called the Gold Coast (present-day Ghana). How many others were involved or knew about the plan the authorities could not determine. At the edge of town the slaves set fire to barns and outhouses. When the fire brigade and neighbors arrived to put out the blaze, the slaves set upon them with firearms, axes, and swords. Some twenty whites were killed or wounded. The culprits fled to the brambles north of the city but were captured the next day. Two committed suicide rather than be taken. Based on the testimony of two slaves caught in the act of setting the fires and taking part in the slaughter of whites, twenty-one slaves were indicted by grand juries and convicted by trial juries. Eighteen were executed. The legal procedure, based on the 1708 statute, itself modeled on that of the freeholders' courts from Barbados, was swift and summary.

One correspondent, reporting on the cases to his superiors in London, noted that "a free Negro who pretends sorcery gave them a powder to rub on their clothes which made them so confident" — a magic potion designed to make the user invisible. He also reported that the conspirators had taken a blood oath not to reveal their plan. Both the use of potions to ensure invisibility or invulnerability and blood oaths were African in origin and appear in a number of other slave uprisings.

The punishment meted out to the convicts was sanguinary and was clearly intended to send a message that every slave and free person of color could not miss. The heads of the executed conspirators were displayed on pikes throughout the city. Today such punishments seem both barbarous and motivated by racial animus. In fact, because the crime was classified as "petty treason" (treason against their masters) rather than arson or murder, the punishment differed little from that imposed in England for treason against the crown.

Perhaps more important than the sanguinary perpetration and outcome of the case were the different ways in which it became part of the lore of slavery in the colony for blacks and whites. Like the city itself, the folklore that grew out of the 1712 events had two faces. For the slaves the story became one of heroic and tragic yearning for freedom. Periodically some slave who remembered or had learned of the 1712 plot would whisper something about it to younger slaves, and the gossip eventually found its way to the authorities. Whites kept the memory of 1712 alive in a different fashion. In 1721 and again in 1730, there were full-blown insurrection scares among whites. They came to nothing, but whites armed themselves and adopted a prison-guard mentality. Though vigorous cross-examination of various slaves would prove the rumors unfounded, the failure to corroborate these plots only fed the anxiety of the authorities. As Horsmanden would later write, they came to believe that the slaves were far better at concealing plots than the whites were at uncovering them.

The response of the authorities to rumored plots was to rewrite the black code to make conspiracy among slaves more difficult. The same merchants and shippers who drafted these laws soon undermined them by importing more slaves and employing them around the city. Given the role of slaves in the city's daily economic life, laws restricting their mobility and assembly were impossible to enforce. The system of passes and patrols that policed slavery on the plantation could not and did not function in the New York City setting. "Self-hires," notably slaves who worked as boatmen on the East and North (Hudson) Rivers and slaves who worked on the docks as carters or drove wagons, all moved about the city in relative freedom. Had they wished, they could have conscripted other slaves into a conspiracy. The relative infrequency of insurrectionary plots should have reassured whites that blacks were not busy planning mayhem, but did not.

Feeding the persistent fears of the authorities was the fact that the conspirators involved in the 1712 cases had chosen arson to begin their rebellion. The city was a tinderbox, its roofs and walls constructed of shingle and planking, its barns full of dry hay, and its warehouses stuffed with alcohol and gunpowder for sale to Indians, for the garrison of soldiers, and for local use. Any fire spelled a potential calamity. Even Fort George, the largest royal military enclosure in the region, was prey to arson, for within its wooden walls were stores of explosives. In his 1738 report to the Board of Trade in England, Lieutenant Governor George Clarke lamented that the fort was "of little defense" to the city or the colony, so vulnerable was it to fire. Were the wind to turn on the city during a raging fire, all property might go up in flames.

For the disgruntled slave, fire had a special attraction. Arson could be an act of resistance, for the initial target was not the poor man's hovel or the slave's quarters but the town houses of the rich and the garrisons of the powerful. Arson was a slave's weapon against the oppressive master, reducing his most valuable property — his home and business — to ashes. Southern masters knew that arson was a time-honored component of all slave rebellions. When whites and blacks arrived to fight the fires, they were vulnerable to ambush. When owners emptied their houses of prized goods to save them from the flames, slaves could steal or destroy the valuables.

Ironically, the most harmful fallout of the conspiracy of 1712 was that the actions of a handful of slaves made it immeasurably harder for all free blacks and all other slaves, particularly those on the verge of manumission, to cross over into the other, better city. The "Negro Act" of 1712, passed after the killers were caught and executed, made social and economic intercourse among blacks even harder. No free black was to give or sell spirits to a slave (even a relative) and no "negro or mulatto" awaiting freedom could own a house or land after they had been freed. The latter provision was intended to prevent slaves and free persons of color from congregating away from the eyes of masters, and plotting or conspiring against them. Each act of desperation by the slaves fueled an equally oppressive legal act, which in turn divided the city even further.

CHAPTER 3

Hotbeds of Crime

Although imagined slave conspiracies always lurked in the shadows, the 1741 crisis did not begin with revelations of a grand conspiracy. Instead, the year opened with reports of a series of thefts and burglaries. The colonial city was always a hotbed of crime, and thriving port cities like New York seemed to attract criminals. Over 50 percent of all crimes reported in the colony took place in the city of New York, a figure vastly out of proportion to the population of the colony. Four times as much theft was recorded in the city as in the outlying counties. Given the colonial lawgivers' obsession with slave conspiracies, one would have expected that slaves constituted a large percentage of the men arrested for crimes. In fact, slaves were tried for crimes in far fewer numbers than their percentage of the population (10 percent of the reported crimes had slave suspects, while slaves represented 18 percent of the city's population). Although some leading scholars have suggested that most slaves' crimes involved theft of their masters' property and that masters punished slaves outside the courts, the relative infrequency of criminal prosecution of slaves also has to do with the nature of the criminal justice system and the types of crimes committed by nonslaves.

Crime plagued the city leaders long before 1741, and no easy answer presented itself. The misperception of epidemic crime levels raised the level of anxiety of the authorities and made them more susceptible to rumors of rampant crime waves and crime rings. One explanation that authorities were inclined to believe was that the diverse backgrounds of those who inhabited the poorer areas of the city made them prone to criminal behavior. From the perspective of modern criminology, one could argue that the demographic structure of New York City did, in fact, play a role in its crime rates, though not as the authorities then supposed. Today we know that most crimes are committed by indigent single men aged seventeen to thirty-five. Studies of crime in early-modern European and American cities suggest the same pattern. New York City in the eighteenth century was home to many young men, including soldiers stationed at the fort, sailors in port, workers at the shipyards and warehouses, craftsmen's apprentices, and servants of the wealthy, not to mention slaves. The closely knit ethnic communities in the city and deeply religious congregations like the French Huguenots and Dutch Reformed had low crime rates because criminal activity was discouraged by ministers, family heads, and respected elders, but many of the poor young men in New York City did not belong to such communities. They had come to the colony alone in search of work, belonged to no church, and were not married.

This demographic picture certainly fit the slaves. Most slaves in the colony were young men. Unlike the white laborers, however, the slaves did not live by themselves. If not part of their masters' families, they formed part of an extended household that included boarders, younger relatives of the master or his family, other slaves, and apprentices. Moreover, the young male slaves were never truly alone. Not only were they watched by their masters, but they were always in the company of other slaves. The romantic notion of slave solidarity inhibiting one slave from informing on the criminal activities of other slaves is unfounded. Slaves were always telling their masters about the misconduct of fellow bondsmen and women.

To explain the motivation of individual criminals, early-eighteenth-century authorities believed that some men and women were simply morally depraved or indifferent to morality. Crime supposedly arose from appetites and passions that morally imperfect men could not control. In effect, this theory held that criminals were born, not made. It was not poverty or want per se that caused crime but moral deformity. The typical criminal was a man without deep social commitments who acted impulsively and repeated crimes throughout his life. A few criminals might reform their ways, but most were incorrigible. In the second half of the eighteenth century, criminologists and penologists like Jeremy Bentham would argue that crime was a social rather than a moral problem, but that a reform movement flowered after the period under study here.

To the master class, the moral depravity theory particularly applied to the slaves — at least according to the view of slave character held by the majority of the master class. As one of the judges at the 1741 conspiracy trials concluded, the African slaves represented a "brutish and bloody species of mankind." They were emotionally immature, impulsive, given to frolic and idleness, untrustworthy, and prone to violence. (Given these traits, why would anyone take an African slave in the household?) But the same slaves were also supposedly childlike, easily forgiven and quick to forget their grievances, happy in their station and beholden to their masters. In the conventional wisdom of the day, slaves lacked the emotional maturity to be fully culpable for their acts yet exhibited an animal nature that could easily motivate them to commit crimes: one more irony of slavery.

Until the reformists' message was understood, the response of authorities to the rising number of crimes was to increase the stakes of criminal activity. Parliament, followed by the colonial legislatures, stiffened penalties for all kinds of grand theft. Stealing a piece of linen from another person's pocket became a capital (death penalty) offense. While one may regard such legislation as class-based — for there can be no doubt that the new criminal laws fell most heavily upon the poor — one must recognize that the purpose of early-modern criminal justice was not just to identify and punish the perpetrators of criminal acts. An equally important purpose was to maintain the social and political status quo.

These two purposes may be at odds. At the end of the movie *Casablanca* the Nazi chief of intelligence has been murdered and the French police chief tells a subordinate to "round up the usual suspects." He knows who has committed the crime and has no intention of exposing him, but social order and the authority of the state must be preserved and that means something must be done. In similar fashion, early-modern criminal justice was sometimes more concerned with the assertion of state power than the exculpation of the wrongly accused.

If much of the authority of the state seemed to revolve around its power to enslave people, the order to round up the usual suspects should have filled the jails with slaves every time a crime was uncovered. To understand why this did not happen under normal circumstances and, conversely, why it did happen in the alleged conspiracy of 1741, we need to know more about the criminal justice system itself and its relation to slavery.

It was not always easy for the magistrates or the courts to demonstrate their puissance in cases of suspected crime. There were no trained forces to police the colonies or to investigate offenses. The entire system was amateurish, ridden with corruption, and poorly run. In the cities a "watch" patrolled at night looking for fires and ordering drunks and disorderly persons off the streets. The watch had no particular expertise in preventing or investigating crimes; moreover, its members were sometimes drawn from the very same groups of people who committed crimes. The cities employed sheriffs (these were patronage appointees) who also had subordinates, but their primary function was serving legal papers on parties to lawsuits. Sometimes sheriffs and undersheriffs were called on to investigate crimes, and they had the power to arrest suspects. They were also responsible for the upkeep of jails, which they did haphazardly. Most colonial jails were cold, damp, disease-ridden, and tumbledown. Inmates reported how easily it was to break out of them. In New York City the basement of the city hall served as the jail, and it was a loathsome place.

The next level of the criminal justice system was the justice of the peace (J.P.). These men were chosen by the crown and given commissions to keep order, hold court, and investigate accusations of crime. They were invariably men of means and often held other elective or appointive office. The J.P.'s own status in the community lent authority to his judgments. Although he was not required to keep a record of his actions — few such records survive — the personal diaries of some of these justices suggest that they relied on a system of fines and bonds that forced neighbors to remain civil toward each other and obey the laws. When it worked, this semiprivate network drew strength from the homogeneity of the community and the hegemonic influence of leading figures in the village or parish. Often these men posted "sureties" that would be forfeited if the offender repeated the offense, indebting the offender to them as they indebted themselves to the court. In addition, this "watch-and-warn" system was cheap to administer.

But neither the system of summonses operated by the sheriffs nor the watch-and-warn system that the J.P.s monitored could maintain order among the slaves. They were not persons in the law and could not be served legal papers. They faced no risk in the forfeit of their sureties' bonds, nor were they likely to need the financial aid of the person who put up the bond. Instead, the sheriff and the J.P.s had to depend upon the cooperation of masters in controlling slaves' misdemeanors. In effect, this privatized the criminal justice system. The result was that few slaves were arrested and turned in for hearings.

The J.P.s in the New York counties also gathered for regular "sessions of the peace" at county courts to hear the presentments of grand juries. These were reports that particular men and women had violated what were called "personal conduct" laws. Subjects of presentment included drunkenness, sexual activity between unmarried people, failure to attend church, and various other misdemeanors that dominated the dockets of these sessions of the peace. It is important to remember that grand juries did not have the same power over the slave. For example, there were no presentments of slaves for fornication. Moreover, masters did not regard their slaves' commission of such infractions as particularly censorious. Finally, the penalty for these offenses was a fine, and since the slaves lacked money, they could not pay for their misdeeds.

The supreme court of the colony heard all cases of "life and limb," that is, serious offenses. The bench of the New York Supreme Court was composed of political figures. They figuratively as well as literally sat at the top of society. Some, like Horsmanden and DeLancey, had formal legal training. With laymen on the high court benches, justice was often swift and sensible. Massachusetts Superior Court justices like Samuel Sewall were deeply moral men, concerned about the quality of their performance. Other colonial judges were not so ethical or capable. Colonial governors like Cosby, doubling as judges, disgraced themselves through venality and partisanship, while men like DeLancey hungered for higher office.

Such men invariably owned slaves and thus had an interest that went far beyond meting out justice in slave criminal cases. On the one hand, they understood well the desire of masters to protect valuable slaves from prosecution. On the other hand, they realized how important it was that the operation of the criminal justice system impress on all slaves the fact that justice would be swift and severe. Thus, the trial, conviction, and gruesome execution of a few slaves for crimes would serve the same purpose as trying many slaves, while not wasting valuable property.

By the same token, slaves in jail awaiting trial or convicted on charges that did not involve insurrection or homicide had an aid which other defendants lacked. Masters were loathe to lose the labor that slaves represented, particularly if the slave had a craft or skill that permitted the master to rent the slave out. Masters consequently peppered the authorities with petitions for pardons of slaves. New York law provided a small repayment to masters for the loss of the slave's value, but masters valued slaves so highly that they sometimes hid them from prosecution or sold them privately before they could be brought to justice. If masters promised to supervise slaves or to sell them out of the colony, their petitions for official mercy were likely to be more effective than a simple plea for mercy. Slaves' capital sentences were often commuted when the master promised to sell the slave. A female slave's pregnancy (called "pleading the belly" at the time) was another category in which judges would automatically offer reprieves if not full commutations.

The supreme court bench also understood the differences between criminal law and procedure for free persons and that for slaves. Over the course of the eighteenth century, criminal law and procedure for free persons had begun to undergo complex changes. On the one hand, the criminal law shifted from a focus on moral and religious matters to economic offenses. In Massachusetts the old Laws and Liberties, with their emphasis on biblical crimes like blasphemy and adultery, gave way to more stringent statutes against forgery, counterfeiting, and theft. In 1718 Pennsylvania, whose first laws stressed social harmony and religious toleration, adopted a criminal code resembling English law. Far harsher penalties against crimes like robbery and burglary were introduced, along with a stricter system of penal bonds.

At the same time as the laws against property offenses stiffened, lawyers for the accused were becoming a prominent feature of colonial criminal courts, anticipating a similar change in English practice by two decades. In New York, leaders of the bar like James Alexander and William Smith agreed to represent free men accused of crimes. In addition, prototypical bills of rights — protecting the right to jury trial, legal counsel, public and speedy hearings of cases, and other familiar procedural guarantees — appeared in over half the colonies. The Massachusetts Body of Liberties (1648), followed by Connecticut's Fundamental Laws (1660), suggested that there was a right to counsel; the Concessions of the West Jersey Proprietors (1677) and the Frame of Government of Pennsylvania (1683) gave the same assurances. The Connecticut General Court followed this practice. Pennsylvania (1718), Delaware (1719), and South Carolina (1731) wrote into their laws explicit provisions for counsel in criminal cases.

New York colonial laws did not provide for lawyers in cases of serious crimes, but its juries did follow the practice of other colonies in routinely asking leniency for first-time offenders and young people. This "jury nullification" of the severity of the law, as it has been called by legal historian William Nelson, would reduce a grand theft to a petty theft.

Since slaves did not have jury trials, they could not benefit from jury nullification, nor did slaves benefit from counsel. For these reasons slaves accused of serious crimes were almost always convicted. Over the long course of colonial rule, defendants in capital cases in Massachusetts, New York, North Carolina, and Virginia were convicted at trial about as often as they were acquitted. In the first half of the eighteenth century conviction rates were lower than in the years leading up to the Revolution. In the seventeenth century women had higher conviction rates than men, but these differences disappeared in the eighteenth century. Rhode Island courts were more lenient than Massachusetts', and Connecticut courts were slightly more likely to convict than Massachusetts courts. Conviction rates in New York varied about a mean of nearly 50 percent, with Dutch, Jews, and free blacks convicted least often.

Slaves were convicted far more often than any other category of suspect — 65 percent compared to 45 percent for whites. This pattern was not uncommon. During the eighteenth century in Richmond County, Virginia, slaves invariably were found guilty of serious crimes. In Massachusetts black servants were twice as likely as white servants to be convicted of major offenses. Masters knew that the criminal justice system would be especially harsh on slaves. Whether for mercenary or sentimental reasons, a master had to think twice before he allowed his slave to face justice in the colonial courts. This clearly reduced the number of slaves that came before the courts.

The deterrent effect of punishments for slaves convicted of crimes may have played a role in the paucity of slaves brought to trial. For the slave convicted of a serious crime, there was a final terror that few other convicts needed to consider. As was previously noted, the law left punishment for certain crimes committed by slaves to the discretion of the courts, and courts often imposed the most horrific sentences. Some slaves convicted in the 1712 arson and murder trials were burned at the stake, one was hanged in chains and left to starve to death, and others were dismembered while alive. If the slave had committed petty treason, that is, if he had murdered his master, the law not only sanctioned but encouraged the most barbarous of punishments as a deterrent to other slaves who might consider such a course. Slaves were present at executions of other slaves. The lesson was a hard one, but perhaps it dissuaded some slaves from crime.

———

Just as the criminal justice system functioned differently for free and slave defendants, so the pattern of their recorded crimes is distinct. That distinction further explains why so few slaves (relative to their numbers) were ever tried. Despite the severity of punishment, criminal law did not deter criminal activity in New York. Historian Douglas Greenberg has compiled a wealth of statistics on crime and criminal prosecution from surviving court records. The average criminal prosecution involved a white male. Over 90 percent of all crimes were committed by men. Only 7.5 percent were committed by blacks. Nearly 90 percent of these latter defendants were slaves. In the city slaves were accused of just over 10 percent of the crimes. English defendants comprised nearly 75 percent of the total number of indictments for crimes, with the Dutch at a little over 13 percent. Other ethnic groups were responsible for a minuscule number of criminal prosecutions.

If the criminal justice system was designed to ferret out slave crimes and operated to the detriment of slaves, why were slaves underrepresented as defendants in court compared to their numbers in the general population? Did they, in fact, commit fewer crimes than white men? Some of the records of criminal courts for the rural counties are missing, but were these records to suddenly appear they would no doubt increase the number of English and Dutch men who were accused of crimes. Few slaves lived on New York's farms.

More clues to the absence of slaves from the records of the criminal courts appear when one breaks down the totals of offenses into four categories: crimes against persons; crimes against property; offenses against public order; and official malfeasance. Men committed nearly 95 percent of all crimes against persons. The vast majority of these were street fights and involved white men. White men committed almost all of the offenses against public order, including contempt of authority of magistrates (for example, riot), and in all cases in which officials were accused of malfeasance. The disproportion of white men's crimes reflects the fact that they, not slaves, held and abused the powers of office, got drunk in public, fought with one another in the streets, and abused the sheriff and his men. These figures, it should be recalled, are for prosecutions. White men were caught while committing these acts because they were willing to engage in public misconduct, much of it at night. The law barred slaves from "night walking."

Turning now to crimes against property, according to court records slaves committed far more crimes against property than against persons. But the combined numbers of recorded violent crimes against persons and crimes against public order outnumbered the thefts, burglaries, robberies, and frauds by a factor of four to one, reducing the relative number of slave defendants.

In New York City slave men were accused of stealing food, clothing, and money. This should not come as a surprise. Southern planters' diaries often complained about slave pilfering. Some historians have argued that these thefts were acts of resistance against the slave system or the result of dire need. Exhumed slave skeletons from the city burial ground show that dietary deficiencies were widespread. Slaves might have stolen food to supplement their diet. Whatever the reason, most of what they took would have been close to hand. This is still the pattern of theft in the city. The master was thus the most likely victim of slave thievery. Most masters were not willing to inform the court that they could not control their slaves. It is impossible to know how often slaves stole from their masters, but one can assume that few of these cases came to trial. Testimony in conspiracy trials also reveals that some masters punished their slaves for theft without reporting it.

Thus, ordinary slave crimes (to coin a phrase) were all but lost in the flood of crimes by white men. And a flood it was. New York City crime rates peaked at ninety prosecuted crimes for every ten thousand adults. These rates were three times higher than in the countryside and over ten times higher than in New England cities. In part New York City's crime rates reflected a restless antipathy toward all forms of authority. Disorderly houses (unlicensed drinking establishments and houses of prostitution) flourished in the face of laws prohibiting their existence, and periodic wars among rival gangs, along with wholesale assaults on warehouses and wharves, made the city a criminal hotbed. Indeed, there was no clear line between private grudges and public crimes in the city. The anger of the white underclasses could just as easily be directed at the city's officials as at one's neighbors or innocent bystanders.

What about the simmering fury of the slaves? Why did it not spill over into crimes? Very likely it did. Modern criminal statistics indicate that most crimes by blacks target other blacks. This includes domestic violence, theft, and rape. But slaves victimized by other slaves reported the offense to their masters or took matters into their own hands rather than turning to the magistrates. Again, the result was fewer slaves formally accused of crime than one might expect.

The paucity of slaves in the docks of the courts did not reassure the aldermen. Perversely, because they expected slaves to be criminals, the authorities were convinced that slaves effectively concealed their crimes. Thus, the relative absence of prosecutions of slaves proved that slaves were adept at hiding their misconduct. As Lieutenant Governor Clarke wrote to the mayor and aldermen of New

York City on January 24, 1742, slaves would always be "cavilling . . . new designs" to commit hidden crimes.

Students of "deviance theory" argue that communities need to use public prosecution of some visible minorities — for example, the Quakers in Massachusetts in the 1650s or the witches of Salem in 1692 and 1693 — to reinstate the values that bind the community together. Persecution of Quakers and witches in seventeenth-century New England restored the harsh conformity and anxious piety of that region. Persecution of slaves for conspiracy served a similar purpose. Every prosecution reminded whites that slavery ultimately depended on force, and that whites must remain vigilant lest the violence they wielded be turned against them. Thus, the difference between conviction rates of whites and blacks for ordinary crimes was a measure not of guilt or innocence but of the necessity for the dominant clique to establish boundaries.

Deviance theory suggests that the authorities' concern with slave crime arose from a more profound prejudice than the assumption that slaves concealed their inveterate misconduct. As suggested above, observers supplied slave motivation from a store of racist assumptions. The authorities assumed that slaves were essentially childlike in their moral capacities but could be stirred by anger and passion. Then, no qualms of conscience would stay their bestial animus. Docile as a rule, their emotions were uncontrollable when aroused. As Justice Frederick Philipse told one of the juries at the sentencing of convicted conspirators, they were "very wicked fellows, hardened sinners, and ripe, as well as ready, for the most enormous and daring enterprises." As Thomas Jefferson opined in a 1781 essay on Virginia, this derived from the slaves' very nature; surface distinctions of color signaled a host of deformities beneath the skin, including sexual ardor, a sensate rather than a reflective nature, and decreased capacity for memory, reason, and imagination.

Assigning to slaves childlike moral natures meant that the authorities could allow their masters to correct their slaves' minor offenses, for these were expected and could not be deterred by public shaming or other formal punishments. But the state must intervene with massive and unyielding force should the slaves' animalistic depravity be unleashed. In such cases the authorities must not allow masters' sympathies to protect slave culprits, for slaves governed by their animal lusts could not be curbed by persuasion. Worst of all, in the minds of the aldermen and judges, when nefarious white confederates stirred the slaves' brutish impulses and directed the slaves in crime, the entire society was at risk. Then the state must act swiftly and decisively to save itself. Niceties of criminal procedure must give way to swift and certain verdicts and exemplary punishments.

The same assumptions about slave mentality and secretiveness that demanded constant watchfulness when slave crime seemed dormant also called for the most strenuous effort of suppression when a conspiracy — particularly one involving whites and blacks — was suspected. What may seem to us today as an overreaction to rumors and unfounded fears is precisely the reaction the criminal justice system was designed to induce among authorities when confronted with evidence of slave conspiracy.

In the winter of 1740–41, the only evidence of a pattern of slave misconduct that the undersheriffs uncovered was that the burglary rate seemed to be rising. Slaves, supposed to be almost invisible at night, were suspected of having had a hand in the thefts, and tavern keeper John Hughson was thought to be the fence for the booty and plunder. His establishment at the end of Crown Street was next to the North (now Hudson) River docks, and items from the warehouses and shops nearby could easily find their way into his possession. It was notorious that slaves used his rooms to drink and gamble after hours. A prostitute named Margaret ("Peg") Kerry could be found there most nights as well.

Hughson was one of many free whites who either courted or at least tolerated the company of slaves. David Brion Davis has called these "independent and irreverent fraternizers" a leaven in the harshness of slavery, and in New York City there were many such men and women. Some acted out of religious conviction, moral concern, simple friendship, or individual esteem and attachment. Others, like Hughson, had a mercenary motive for fraternization. Not only were the slaves his customers, they were his confederates in crime.

Most of what we know about Hughson and the doings in his tavern is derived from the testimony of his patrons following his indictment for receiving stolen goods. The testimony is often contradictory and some of it is perjured as well. A capable modern defense attorney would be able to punch enough holes in it to raise a reasonable doubt in the minds of jurors. But most historians who have studied these records agree that Hughson was running a criminal operation. His patrons included a criminal crew calling itself the Geneva Club (named after the Dutch jenever, or gin, they had stolen from a warehouse on the docks some years before). It was headed by a slave, Caesar Varick, and his friends, Cuffee Philipse and Prince Auboyneau. They were also known as the Long Bridge Boys.

The Geneva Club was interested in eating, drinking, boasting, whoring, and crime, but there were those who patronized Hughson's who had deeper grievances against the English. They included Spanish-speaking sailors like Wan or Juan, members of the crew of a "prize" — a Spanish ship captured by a New Yorker and brought into New York's port. Such prizes — consisting of the ship, cargo, and sailors — could be held or sold. The sailors insisted that they were free men and demanded that they be treated as prisoners of war and exchanged for captured colonists or Britons. The prize master refused and sold them as slaves. These men knew all about slave rebellions in the Caribbean and wanted to return to their homelands.

Joining them at Hughson's long tables during those smoke-filled, boisterous nights were older English-speaking house slaves like Jack Comfort, who knew about the 1712 revolt and exaggerated its carnage with every telling. White visitors like Irishman William Kane, a soldier stationed at the fort, discussed the war between England and Spain and worried aloud that they might be sent to fight in the disease-ridden semitropics where the war raged. Others at these gatherings had learned of the Stono Rebellion of 1739. In it, over a hundred slaves marched through the colony of South Carolina on their way to freedom in Spanish Florida, killing whites and torching houses along the way. The colonial militia defeated the slave band in a pitched battle and summarily executed many slaves thought to be involved, but the colony remained terrified of the prospect of another rebellion. Hughson's regular customers might be demeaned by upstanding New Yorkers as the "outcasts of many nations," but they were not ignorant of the conflicts and injustices in the world.

Hughson's tavern was watched by the authorities, for they suspected that sinister doings occurred there. On occasion the under-sheriff would enter unannounced, hoping to find stolen goods in plain sight. Other establishments like Hughson's were raided as well. Peter "the Doctor," one of the suspects in the 1712 arson case, was later arrested for hosting a regular gathering of slaves and free persons at which crime was a favored topic. John Romme's nearby dramshop was also searched.

What appeared sinister to the magistrates was a home away from home to the patrons. Even for the better sort of client, taverns were the one place in the colonies where distinctions of wealth and family and racial prejudices were dissolved by alcohol. Late at night, with smoke curling up from pipes and the odor of whiskey and rum in the air, the tavern beckoned. In this winter the nights were especially cold, for it was the final stage of what climatologists have called "the little ice age." The Hudson River had been frozen most of the winter and firewood was in short supply. Part of the allure of even the meanest taverns was their roaring fireplaces.

The gatherings at Hughson's were occasions for conviviality in the freest social atmosphere of the entire city. Men exhausted by work, as well as those who were full of guile and mischief, nursing grudges against unfeeling bosses and brutal masters, gambled, ate, drank, danced, and toasted one another. They could also flirt with the women of the establishment, including Hughson's wife, his daughter, and the ubiquitous Peg. Mary Burton later admitted that she resented the lascivious attention paid her as she performed her duties. Sometimes these whispered promises of affection led to liaisons. Caesar Varick and Peg had a child in the fall of 1740.

For the elite, power meant property, finery, status, family connections, and political influence. The regulars at Hughsons, both slave and free, had none of these. What they had instead was talk. Did the talk include plans to overthrow the colony itself? The prosecution tried to prove this at the trials. A little speculation may be in order since human nature has not changed all that much in the intervening years. Alcohol still loosens the tongue. Male hormones still cause young men in their cups to engage in can-you-top-this boasts. Then as now the drinkers boasted of feats of strength and cunning. They told stories and sang songs about far-off places they had known as home or ports of call. They exchanged tales of sexual prowess. It would not have been unthinkable for them to have spun grandiose schemes for revenge and revolt. The target probably varied from night to night, depending on who was leading the conversation. For the Spanish-speaking African sailors, it was sea captain John Lush, who had taken their ship not far from its Cuban port and had carried them to this inhospitable place. For the Irish off-duty soldiers it was their hated sergeants and the notorious discipline of the English army. For slaves like Caesar Varick, Quaco Walters, and Cuffee Philipse, it was their masters, merchants John Varick and John Walters, and Adolph Philipse, a member of the governor's council and one of the leading men in the colony, who flaunted their wealth by purchasing lavish mansions, carriages, and elegant clothing.

Did Hughson's regulars realize that such words put their heads in the noose? The difference in law between mere talk and criminal conspiracy was a fine one. It varied according to who was speaking and what was being said. If the white dockworkers got drunk and discussed how they would like to rid themselves of their betters, there was no conspiracy but merely an "attempt," and for persecution this required some act in furtherance of the plot. If the slaves at Hughson's uttered the same words, they were liable to serious penalties. If whites like Hughson encouraged slaves in criminal conversations, they faced a similar punishment.

Even if Hughson and his band of thieves knew about these legal distinctions, they assumed that the anonymity of their late-night meetings and their oaths to one another never to reveal the contents of their conversations would protect them. According to later testimony, these oaths sometimes involved bloodletting modeled on African secret-society initiations. On other occasions, the conspirators admitted, they had sworn fidelity on Hughson's Bible.

While the denizens of Hughson's muttered darkly, the newspapers carried accounts of the Stono Rebellion, uprisings in the West Indies, and other slave insurrections. The language of the reports verged on the hysterical. From it one might assume that the whites sensed the arrival of Judgment Day, but this would be incorrect. Events in South

Carolina and the Caribbean seemed far away from the city. It took many weeks and even months for news from distant places to reach New York. The stories ended up on the back pages, alongside advertisements for imported books and clothing. The whites of the city were vaguely aware of the danger of slave insurrections, but its prospect was far more vivid for the slaves at Hughson's.

When mere words become crimes, there is no limit to the discretion of the authorities to single out and punish a disgruntled minority. Fearing slave conspiracies and possessing the power to enforce a discriminatory conspiracy law, New York officials could have swooped down on dens of suspected criminals, like those at Hughson's, and summarily convicted the slaves under the conspiracy law. It should be recalled that no jury was necessary; freeholders' courts heard cases of slave crimes. Evidence for the conspiracy could have been manufactured, but that was not necessary, for slaves would have willingly informed on one another to gain the favor of the court. Under the law, slaves were permitted to testify about other slaves' statements and actions. If slaves refused to speak, the court could always proffer freedom to the first slave to accuse his comrades. (In such cases masters were compensated out of the public treasury.) It had all been done before and would be repeated in colonial courts. The New York case was different, however. It was not concocted by panicky or sinister inquisitors. The conspiracy really occurred. But what was its aim, and who were its participants?

CHAPTER 4

Where There's Smoke . . .

During that long, cold winter of 1740–41, idle talk at Hughson's about killing masters and turning society upside down so that slaves would be on top finally led to action. Why then? Peter Linebaugh and Marcus Rediker's *Many-Headed Hydra*, the most recent study of class unrest in the early-modern Atlantic world, proposes that slave rebellions were part of a larger phenomenon. They were merely one form of protest by means of which the lower orders asserted their resistance to the authority of the upper classes — "a conspiracy by a motley proletariat." To be sure, the slave colonies in the West Indies were plagued by such uprisings. Dutch Guiana (Surinam) had a major revolt every decade. English Jamaica's "maroon wars" between white militia and runaway slaves were ongoing. Antigua exploded in 1736, leaving many whites and blacks dead. But the mainland colonies did not experience such general uprisings. The Stono Rebellion of 1739 in South Carolina was the only episode that matched the West Indian uprisings.

The New York conspiracy was not part of a general movement. It did not represent the clash of transcendent or fundamental forces. Instead, it was localized and contingent upon a multitude of overlapping small causes. None of these prior events was necessary; none had to happen. No irresistible historical process preordained that the conspiracy would occur. Had any of the principals not acted as he or she did on a number of occasions, the conspiracy would have been stillborn. Had two of the Geneva Club gang not bullied their way into a burglary that a ship's white cabin boy had planned to undertake himself, the conspiracy would never have come to light. Had an officer at the fort not barred a slave from visiting with his wife (she was a cook at the fort) in the evenings, none of the conspirators would have done anything in furtherance of their words.

There were those in the city underworld who were not members of the gangs. One of these was a ship's boy named Christopher Wilson, a teenager "belonging to the Flamborough man of war" that patrolled the coast beyond the harbor. Evidently he had too much time on his hands while his ship was in port, possessed a keen eye for others' valuables, and had little money in his pocket. Sometime before the end of February 1741 (it would have been 1740–41 according to the old-style calendar still in use in the colony) Wilson overheard two white servants employed at the home of merchant Robert Hogg say that Mrs. Hogg kept Spanish milled coins in the drawer of the shop. He took a look for himself when he and another crew member were in the shop buying linens. On the night of February 28, 1741, the coins disappeared.

Wilson may have done the deed himself, or passed on the information to Caesar Varick, Prince Auboyneau (a slave belonging to John Auboyneau) and Cuffee Philipse. At the very least, they wanted a portion of Wilson's booty, and he promised them a share, all the while resenting their assertiveness. Wilson notified Hughson that he would be receiving the coins shortly. Soon Peg knew of the plot, along with fence John Romme, whose shop was nearby, as did just about everyone else who frequented Hughson's establishment. (There were few secrets among these men and women — hardly the best atmosphere for concocting a conspiracy.)

Remembering Wilson's interest in her money drawer, the next day Mrs. Hogg accused Wilson of the theft, and he told the sheriff that a soldier named John Gwin, or Quinn, had shown him some of the coins the night before at Hughson's. The sheriff assumed that Quinn was one of the Irish soldiers from the garrison that lodged with Hughson. In fact, Gwin and Quinn were among the aliases used by Caesar Varick. The aliases that Caesar and other slaves, like Varick's slave Bastian (also known as Tom Peal), used raise tantalizing questions about identity. Who knew Caesar Varick as John Gwin? Certainly not Varick himself. Instead, the aliases were part of a code that had meaning within the subculture of criminal gangs in the city. The code name protected the individual should someone overhear the gang members or their confederates plotting. Within his gang and among criminals who frequented Hughson's, Caesar was Gwin.

Peg had her own list of names, including Irish Peg, Newfoundland Peg, Negro Peg, Margaret Kerry, Margaret Sorubiero, and Margaret Salingburgh. (The latter may have been two variants of the same name, that of her former husband.) Peg, who could not write her own name and had to have her confessions read back to her, was probably illiterate. The former names charted her life's journey from Ireland, to Newfoundland, to a liaison with Caesar Varick. They were not gang names but rather markers of her descent into prostitution. The names told a story of the movement of poor whites from Ireland and Scotland around the North Atlantic empire, a mirror image of the flow of slaves from Africa to the Caribbean that brought the "Spanish Negroes" to New York. They, too, had gained new names like William and John, English equivalents of the names their Spanish masters had given them. Wilson was playing the naming game by referring to Caesar as Gwin. In fact, Wilson already had his own nickname, Yorkshire, perhaps a recollection of his birthplace.

On March 1, after having found no man named Quinn at Hughson's, the sheriff pressured Wilson a little harder, and he revealed that Caesar Varick and Prince Auboyneau were the culprits. That same day Caesar was examined and jailed, though he denied all accusations. He must have been furious with Wilson for betraying whatever part he had played in the theft. Prince was arrested the next day. Both men already had criminal records for theft, which meant that a conviction on this charge would likely cost them their lives. The fact that Wilson was white worried them since his testimony in court would carry far more weight than their denials. The racial divide, until then all but invisible in the tavern, had reappeared. The two men believed that Hughson, whose trust they had taken for granted, would be the next to point a finger at them. By the end of the week, he did, admitting that he had "seen" some of the purloined items in the slaves' hands.

The truly devastating evidence against the two slaves came from Mary Burton, a coquettish sixteen-year-old servant to Hughson. Those historians who dismiss the conspiracy charges find her testimony particularly problematic. She was young enough to be intimidated by the bearing and status of the men who wanted her to testify against the slaves, but if one believes Horsmanden's account of how she became a witness, it does not reveal a child who sought the approval of powerful adults. Instead, she was a tease.

At first her revelations concerned the burglary, not the conspiracy. On March 3, while engaged in a casual conversation with the Kannadys, whose store she frequented to buy candles for Hughson (the nighttime doings at the tavern must have required a good many candles, and candles were not cheap), Burton let slip that she knew more than anyone about the crime. The Kannadys flew to the sheriff with the news, and he and his undersheriff examined Burton closely. At first she denied having intimated anything about the crime to the Kannadys. Then she wept, fearing that she would be killed "by Hughson or the Negroes" if she told the truth. Finally she accused them of plotting all manner of mischief. What she actually said was that she had seen them together and had overheard them talking. It is highly unlikely that she knew that their conversations about anything other than theft were in any way criminal. That is, she did not realize, until after she was told by the men examining her, that mere words amounted to crimes. Once she knew this, the character of her testimony changed. Indeed, it does (for us, though not for Horsmanden) become more problematic as evidence. In other words, once she knew the power she wielded over others, she grew bolder and more certain of what she had heard and seen.

Did she ever speak the truth, even as she understood it? Or were the words put in her mouth by men of influence who had long sought to break up the Geneva Club and put Hughson out of business? Did she speak out of fright? There was, at this stage, no prospect of gain, for the common council and the governor did not offer a reward for information about the conspiracy to commit arson until the middle of April — nearly six weeks after they had heard Burton's revelations. In November, when all the trials were over, she would claim and gain that reward.

Should the authorities have considered her (as they eventually did) a reliable witness? The men who led her through her testimony wanted her to reveal all that she knew, but they had sworn her to tell the truth, and they did not want her to invent details. In the coming trials nothing that she said was enough — that is, without corroboration by other witnesses or confession by at least two defendants — to convict anyone. In a way, the authorities' predisposition against the suspects matched her growing assertiveness, for they truly believed there was a widespread conspiracy. Still, at first they were doubtful of her veracity. She switched from tease to tears too easily. At the same time, she was the only witness they had who had first-hand knowledge of what had transpired inside Hughson's, and they pumped her for information.

Her first revelation was that Caesar Varick and Peg were sleeping together. Peg had given birth the previous fall. Her infant was dark in color, and Caesar, still in custody, conceded that he was Peg's lover. This admission gave credence to at least part of Burton's testimony. More was confirmed on March 4 when Hughson produced some of the stolen goods, which he claimed had been secreted in his establishment without his knowledge. He blamed John Romme, who had inconveniently fled. And there the matter stood until the mysterious fire of March 18 at the fort, when the plot thickened.

––––––

The phrase "the plot thickens" is a cliché in mystery stories, but here it has many legitimate meanings. First, after the theft at the Hoggs' store, the authorities' knowledge of the slaves' plot increased. They discovered that it involved more than just the Long Bridge gang and its rival, Smith's Fly Boys, and entailed more than a simple snatch-and-run operation. The whites' fears of a slave insurrection, hitherto a kind of free-floating anxiety, would soon become palpable and widespread. It is at this point that Horsmanden's journal begins, with its many intersecting story lines involving both black and white protagonists.

Although it was intended as a kind of official transcript, one should also read the journal as a work of nonfiction. Viewed in this way, it is not just an official record or a single person's point of view but rather the source of many stories — almost too many. There is Horsmanden's, to be sure, but there are also those of others: suspects and witnesses that talk to us; confessors drawing upon what they saw and heard, what they believed, and what they thought their audience wanted to hear; prosecutors like the pitiless and narrow-minded William Smith and judges like the politically adept James DeLancey — each with their own agendas.

All the stories came together on the night of March 18, 1741.

The fire that overtook Fort George was clearly visible throughout the city. It seemed to begin everywhere: from the roof, where repairs were under way, it spread to the governor's mansion, the chapel, and the armory. The recorder's office atop the gate was totally destroyed. The state papers stored within were dumped on the street. The thought of official records of the colony scattered about the ash-covered cobblestones — which the recorder had compiled and for which he was responsible — infuriated and saddened Horsmanden.

The billowing smoke from the roof of the fort's magazine sent the fire brigades scurrying to the scene. A raging wind prevented the bucket brigade and the pumpers from putting out the fire, but a saving rainstorm prevented the fire from spreading beyond a building or two outside the fort's walls. As Horsmanden reported to the city's common council, the fire had "entirely destroyed" the secretary's office. He sought permission to move his operations to another building.

Was it an accident? At first it was attributed to a repairman's faulty soldering iron. Later deponents, including whites and slaves, would aver that the slave Quaco Roosevelt set the fire to pay back the lieutenant governor for not letting him visit his new wife, a cook at the fort; Quaco would admit as much on the eve of his execution for the arson. For him the fire served as a modicum of revenge against a system that separated him from a loved one.

But he had not stopped at personal gratification. Before he slipped into the fort to set his fire, he had talked others into joining a wider plan to torch the city. Such a plan fit Hughson's and Caesar Varick's scheme to rob homes while their owners were out fighting fires. In the three weeks after March 18, Quaco's single incendiary act became a contagion of fires — some thirteen in all. On March 25 Captain Warren's roof caught fire. On April 1 a fire began in Winant Van Zant's storehouse. Three days later hay stored in the barn of a certain Mr. Vergereau, who owned a boardinghouse, started smoldering, and no sooner was it extinguished than fire was discovered in the kitchen loft of Ben Thomas's house. In the April 4 fires the fire brigade discovered hot coals nestled in the dry hay. The next day glowing coals were discovered under a haystack next to Joseph Murray's barn, and a trail of soot led to a neighbor's house. On Monday,

April 6, the city awoke to three fires, the most serious of which, at Philipse's warehouse, could have turned into a conflagration had the fire brigade not arrived so swiftly. One member of the brigade saw a black man jumping out of the far window of the warehouse as the firefighters arrived. The other two fires adjoined the home of Captain Jacob Sarly, who had purchased at auction one of the Afro-Spanish sailors Captain Lush had brought back from his privateering voyage.

The town was roused and rumor soon turned to panic. A woman recalled that she had heard three slaves talking animatedly in the street. One said, "Fire, fire, scorch, scorch. A little damn it, bye and bye," then threw up his hands and laughed. He was later identified as Quaco Walters. The targeting of Sarly's house induced some to cry out "the Spanish Negroes, take up the Spanish Negroes" that had been sold to Sarly by Captain Lush. Cuffee Philipse was identified as the man leaping from his master's burning warehouse. The aldermen, meeting at city hall on April 6, reviewed the rumors and accusations and decided there was merit to them, for "many people had . . . terrible apprehensions upon this occasion." How Horsmanden knew this one cannot tell. Perhaps he projected his own fears on others or read the truth in the faces of the tired firemen as they raced from alarm to alarm. He attended the city hall meeting and approved the arrest and interrogation of Quaco Walters. But Walters was as clever in the face of the inquisition as he had been incautious in the street. He admitted what he had been overheard to say but insisted that he was referring to the taking of Puerto Bello from the Spanish by the English fleet. Welcome news of the victory had come to the city earlier, and the aldermen were satisfied that Quaco's story was plausible and let him go. In the meantime Hughson and his wife were sent to jail for receiving stolen goods. The authorities had not yet heard about a conspiracy from Mary Burton, but that did not stop the whites in the city from accusing the blacks of the worst imaginable crimes.

Historians have proposed a variety of explanations as to why rumor and gossip — staples of communication, community life, and entertainment in close-knit societies like eighteenth-century New York City — so easily lent themselves to panic-based accusations. There are numerous examples of such panic in America's early history, where the supernatural and the factual mingled. For example, in the Salem panic of 1692 eyewitnesses swore that witches flew through the air to black masses at which the devil presided. The faces of the witches were familiar, for they were the witnesses' own neighbors. In times of panic, accusations came easily, and the likely target was the "outside agitator," the stranger, the newcomer, the marginal member of the community. Thus, at the very outset of the arson epidemic in New York City, the common council of the city warned against "strangers lurking about the city" who might "have opportunities of pilfering and plundering," and the lieutenant governor ordered the militia "to stop all suspected persons" fitting this description.

In this case the panic within the white community almost immediately focused on the black population, with "the negroes" the repeated cry. Lieutenant Governor Clarke mustered the soldiers at the fort to join an enlarged night watch and ordered a "general search" of the slaves' dwellings to uncover evidence of stolen goods. Little was found, but in the rooms of Robin Chambers and his wife Cuba the searchers found clothing they considered "improper for, and unbecoming the condition of slaves, which made [them] suspect they were not come honestly by." The burden of proof lay with the slaves to explain how they had obtained such "unbecoming" garments, and they were arrested.

Slaves, the authorities implied, should know their debased station. In effect, the magistrates were subjecting the slaves to the old English idea of sumptuary regulation. Under laws passed in the sixteenth century, individuals who were not of a sufficiently high station could not wear certain kinds of expensive apparel or decoration. These laws had come over to the colonies but were rarely enforced or had been allowed to lapse. Yet the aura of the laws persisted, and they were applied to Robin and Cuba.

Slaves did not bow to this discriminatory application of the law. Instead, they delighted in fancy coats, stylish hats, and a rainbow of striking colors in their attire. As Shane White and Graham White have documented in their book entitled *Stylin'*, slaves deliberately affected contrasts in patterns and colors to make a vivid impression on one another. The searchers no doubt were aware of these trends in slave haberdashery but did not care. That slaves would possess costumes "unbecoming" to their station must be proof of crime. As Lieutenant Governor Clarke would remark a year later, the "arrogance" of such slaves was galling to their masters.

The city council met on April 11, 1741, and Horsmanden took the lead in arguing that the fires must be the work of "some villainous confederacy of latent enemies among us." It may be that Horsmanden's recollection of the meeting, in particular his introduction of the term "confederacy," was a convenient hindsight. The minutes of the common council are silent on who actually used the term "confederacy," if it was uttered at all, and Horsmanden's assumption of leadership cannot be verified. But he was also on the colony council, and he surely reported in 1741 (as he recalled in 1744) that the colonial government was "watchful, and anxious for the safety of the city." He reminded the mayor and aldermen seated around the table that the governor could offer a reward but that the city must fund it. The council agreed to offer a reward of one hundred pounds for any free person supplying information about a suspected arson conspiracy. "And any slave that shall make such discovery to be manumitted (freed by the owner) or made free. And the master of such slaves to receive £25 therefore. And the slave to receive £20 and be pardoned." If the informant was a free negro, the reward was to be forty-five pounds and a pardon. Mayor John Cruger and Horsmanden repaired to the lieutenant governor's mansion and presented him with the proposal and the promise that the city would pay the reward.

Clarke acceded to the council's request, and on April 17, 1741, he announced the bounty for such information. Such bounties are common today; the one for the terrorist leader Osama bin Laden topped five million dollars. In the eighteenth century many criminal proceedings ("qui tam") began with an informant's report. For example, in customs violation cases the informant split with the court the value of the smuggled goods confiscated from the defendant. Offers of this sort were not only economically advantageous to the colony and the crown (payment came out of the offender's own pocket) but necessary. The informant, often a kind of professional inquiry agent, simply reported to the crown prosecutors or the justices of the peace in the locality. The council and the lieutenant governor hoped that an offer of monetary reward for free persons and freedom for slaves would break the code of silence and reveal the scope and perpetrators of the "confederacy."

In the meantime, Cuffee Philipse was closely examined and his continued silence about what he was doing in the warehouse when it caught fire only whetted the aldermen's curiosity. On April 21 he was bound over to answer to the grand jury assembled by the regular session of the supreme court of the colony. There the jurymen — some of them, like Van Zant, victims of the fires; others, masters of slaves — and John Cruger Jr., the mayor's son, listened to Frederick Philipse, one of the justices of the court, warn of the "many frights and terrors" which the arson had caused. Philipse concluded that the fires were "not mere chance" but the work of "premeditated malice and wicked pursuits of evil and designing persons." The grand jury was to ferret out the ringleaders "by all lawful ways and means." At the same time, Philipse wanted the grand jury to help put a stop to the selling of rum and other strong liquor "to Negroes." If the grand jurors had not already made the connection between the arson and the usual suspects, Philipse made sure to underscore the point: slaves were notorious for both their drunkenness and their conspiratorial nature. Lastly, Philipse reminded the grand jurors that they could begin with the slaves jailed for the robbery at the Hoggs'.

It was not a slave who broke down and told all to the court on April 22 — at least, not at first — but Mary Burton. Initially she was unwilling to testify under oath before the grand jury; she would not even come into the room voluntarily. Horsmanden made a fuss and insisted she must tell all at once. Burton was still troubled, uneasy, and did not want to speak. The lieutenant governor's proclamation that was read to her did not loosen her tongue. She "despised it," she said. She waved away the promise of protection from the perpetrators. Only the threat of jail changed her mind. The difficulty she had in testifying proved to Horsmanden that she spoke the truth, but he should have been more circumspect, for what she said that day was different from what she had ventured a month and a half earlier.

According to Horsmanden, Burton told the grand jury that she would depose on oath what had happened at the Hoggs' store "but would say nothing about the fires." Her slip of the tongue "much alarmed the grand jury." Indeed, it was providential, Horsmanden opined (again with benefit of hindsight), for it induced the jurymen to "use their utmost diligence to sift out the discovery." Still, she coquettishly withheld it until pressed with "recourse to religious topics." She would have to answer to God for her silence. Faced with damnation, she told all. Indeed, the words tumbled out. Horsmanden's usual restrained prose gave way to the frenzied blank verse of Burton's torrent of fearful memories. Even his grammar broke down as he recorded her fevered recollections.

She claimed to have overheard everything. Prince Auboyneau and Caesar Varick had brought the stolen coins from Hogg's place to Hughson's. Together with Cuffee Philipse, they had met frequently at Hughson's and had often talked of burning down the fort — and the whole town besides — and the fact that the Hughsons had offered as much assistance as they could. During these conversations, Caesar styled himself the next governor, Hughson would be appointed king, and Cuffee asserted that he would be rich as soon as the town was ablaze and all the whites in it murdered. To this end they had obtained seven or eight guns and some swords. Burton recounted that "twenty or thirty Negroes" had met at one time in her master's house and plotted this insurrection, and the ringleaders swore that they would burn her alive if she uttered a word to anyone of what they had said.

The grand jury was "amazed" and rushed to the court, which resumed its session in a somber mood. Courts have immense discretion but little actual power. They depend upon a handful of officers to enforce their judgments and beyond that, the support of the citizenry. An important part of that body is the bar, and the justices immediately summoned the leading lawyers in the city — Smith, Chambers, Murray, and Alexander — to consult with them on procedure.

———

The proceedings now took on another dimension, quite apart from the ferreting out of a criminal conspiracy. Some lawyers summoned to aid the court, like Smith, were former Morris faction leaders. Others among the prosecution, like Attorney General Bradley, were beholden to Cosby. But as Bradley said to the court when the trials began, "This is a cause of very great expectation, it being, as I conceive, a matter of the utmost importance that ever yet came to be tried in this province." Divided by a contest over the spoils of office in the 1730s, the fear of slave conspiracy in the 1740s now united the white power structure to face a common enemy.

It is often true that criminal law and prosecution for crime perform an integrating function in a society, defining its boundaries and identifying those who deviate from the norms imposed by its leaders. Thus, a folk doctor becomes a witch when he or she kills instead of healing, and a privateer becomes a pirate when he stops following the letter of his commission and starts preying on all ships that cross his path. The slave conspiracy grew more real in the eyes of the jurors, judges, and prosecutors because it provided the occasion for a restatement of their common values. These included stern religious ideas, the defense of property, and the belief in the superiority of the English way of life.

The lawyers suggested — and the court agreed — that the slaves should not be tried summarily in freeholders' courts, though the law provided for just such a hearing in cases of suspected conspiracy. Instead, the slaves would be brought before the grand jury, bound over on indictments, tried before a petty jury, allowed to call witnesses, all before the supreme court. This was necessary to find out if there were whites who were party to the plan. All of the members of the bar agreed to take turns serving as special prosecutors.

Horsmanden insisted that the reason for the deviation from the law was the severity of the case and the possible involvement of whites, but there was another reason to take the rumored conspiracy to the supreme court instead of a special freeholders' court. The freeholders' courts for slaves had come under criticism after the 1712 trials, and lawyers like Horsmanden were not only thin-skinned about such criticism but realized that on occasion it was merited. What is more, the justices were after other game besides vengeful slaves: they wanted to round up the Hughson crew. This meant that they would need the testimony of slaves against Hughson. By law slaves could not testify against a white person in a freeholders' court. To change the law for this case would have opened a Pandora's box. So the justices simply convened a grand jury to hear slaves' testimony against whites. Finally, a grand jury indictment and trial before the supreme court gave the judges the maximum chance of turning sullen defendants into willing witnesses for the prosecution. The full might of the state would be displayed to the defendants in such proceedings, and with the possibility of a pardon (under the lieutenant governor's proclamation) as a carrot to go with the stick, the full extent of the conspiracy could be unraveled.

None of this seemed to impress Peg. Confronted with Mary Burton's testimony, Peg denied everything. Offered the possibility of a pardon "if she deserved it," she declared that she would not falsely accuse the innocent. Arraigned on the indictment of the grand jury for the burglary at Hogg's place, Caesar Varick and Prince Auboyneau pleaded not guilty. Horsmanden's hopes for a swift resolution of the matter were dashed. The problem now was how to gather evidence beyond Burton's accusations. The price of holding show trials in the supreme court instead of swift ones in the freeholders' courts was the accumulation of sufficient evidence to convince a trial jury that the men and women standing before it were guilty.

The modern standard of such conviction is "beyond reasonable doubt." Even today these words have contested meanings and judges give varying instructions to juries as to how to interpret the phrase, but in the mid-eighteenth century there was no such formula. Instead, judges instructed juries to find verdicts "upon good conscience," which meant a discerning sifting of fact from falsehood. There was no bar to the introduction of hearsay into evidence, or of pure speculation by witnesses. Hearsay and speculation could be lurid and entirely without corroboration. Judges did not weed it out, and jurors could credit what they heard or dismiss it as they wished.

Finally, there were no defense lawyers to prepare alternative readings of testimony or to persuade juries of the contradictions, illogic, or prejudice in the prosecution witnesses' testimony. Lawyers could participate, but the state did not provide free defense counsel to the indigent as it does today. Slaves could not afford lawyers. Although the scales were weighted against the defendants, they still might escape conviction if the prosecution could not find anyone other than Burton to swear that they were part of a conspiracy.

So the court delayed the trials from April 25 — when Caesar, Prince, the Hughsons, and Peg were first scheduled to be tried —

until May 1, hoping that one of the defendants confined in the jail would break. The jails themselves might persuade the defendants to change their tune. The city jail was in the bowels of the hall where the common council met. If family or friends on the outside did not provide food and bedding, or pay the jailer, the prisoner went without. In the summer the inmates sweltered. In the winter they froze. The winter of 1740–41 was one of the worst that anyone could remember, and a second bout of freezing weather visited the city in the early spring. There was barely enough firewood for those who could afford it and none for the prisoners. Surely they would soon begin to trade their silence for the mercy of the court.

CHAPTER 5

"Voluntary and Wicked Acts"

On May 1, Caesar Varick and Prince Auboyneau stood before the trial jury on indictments for the burglary at Hogg's place and another burglary at Abraham Meyers Cohen's shop on March 1. Both pleaded not guilty. The prosecution and the slaves each presented their cases to the jury, which retired and returned with its verdict. Although the slaves did not have legal counsel — nor did they have alibis — they were able to get three of the aldermen, including Prince's master John Auboyneau, to give them general character references.

Character witnesses played a vital role in capital trials, particularly when the prosecution could not produce witnesses to testify to the fact that the defendants performed the criminal act in question. Friends, family, coworkers, ministers, and magistrates could all be summoned to court to give a defendant a good character reference, but slaves never summoned other slaves since the court would dismiss such character witnesses as unreliable. Character witnesses had more weight then than now because they testified under oath — and people took oaths more seriously then — but slaves could never testify under oath.

Witnesses for the crown included the victims, Burton, and Wilson. Wilson's testimony is neither recorded nor summarized. Horsmanden's account only grew detailed when the charges involved the arson conspiracy. Most likely Wilson had made a deal with the prosecution. Peg also testified for the prosecution. On April 22 the grand jury had indicted her as an accessory to the theft. At that time she refused to admit her complicity or accuse anyone else of the crime, but she had evidently changed her mind by May 1. The lawful penalty for two counts of burglary was death by hanging. The court did not, however, immediately pronounce that sentence. The judges wanted to hear what Caesar and Prince knew about the arson plot.

One cannot know what they were thinking, but the court had implied that Caesar and Prince might still bargain for their lives by naming co-conspirators in the arsons. This is what Peg feared most. Having contributed her small bit to the conviction of Caesar and Prince, Peg became nervous. She feared that they would name her as a party to the conspiracy. Two days after the trial she confided in Arthur Price, a servant jailed for trying to run off with some of the household goods removed from Clarke's mansion during the fire. (He took Clarke's goods at night from a house where they were stored.) If the two condemned slaves denounced her, she would reveal the full extent of the arson conspiracy. According to Price, she whispered, "There is fourteen sworn . . . about the fire."

The next day Peg told Price that Burton "had made me as black as the rest," meaning, one supposes, that Peg had learned that Burton had linked her to the conspiracy. Neither Price nor Peg noticed that the phrase she used and he repeated was one of the casual ways in which the English language linked the color black to evildoing, nor that "black as the rest" also implied that color was a badge of infamy. Price and Peg both realized that her conviction was assured. Now she wanted "revenge on them." Price relayed the conversations to the sheriff, who shared them with the judges. Like Wilson, Price was dealing. As far as one can tell from the surviving records, his burglary never came to trial.

On May 6 Peg was tried together with the Hughsons for receiving stolen goods. Attorney General Bradley and counselor James Murray (it was his turn as special counsel) led the prosecution. Once more it took the jury a single session to hear the evidence for the prosecution and the defense, retire, and return with a guilty verdict. In the meantime Arthur Price, seeking to have his own case reduced or dismissed, had become a full-time investigator for the court and was working undercover. He had chatted up Sarah Hughson, daughter of the convicted tavern keeper, in the jail, where she revealed that a fortune-teller had warned her of troubles to come. It would not have been difficult for the fortune-teller to know that Hughson's entire family was under suspicion. Price led Sarah on. Was she not aware of the plot of the slaves? "No," she said, but he reported that she "colored," put on and took off her bonnet, and asked him "if he knew who it was and when he had heard it." She supposed that the informant was Dundee Todd, a "black dog" so mistrusted by his master that he was scheduled to be sold away from the colony. She would not inform on her parents, however, and would not aid in the investigation. In her fantasy world she dreamed of going "up into the country," thereby escaping all her travails. In the meantime, the men who persecuted her "would have a great deal more damage and danger in [New] York, than they were aware of." Despite her refusal throughout the summer to confess or to condemn her parents, thereby repeatedly displeasing the court, Sarah Hughson would escape the noose. To accomplish this she would have to perjure herself and condemn an innocent man to death.

On May 7 Peg kept her promise to Price. She confessed to the undersheriff that she had seen twelve slaves at John Romme's house, including Caesar Varick and Cuffee Philipse, and that "they proposed to burn the fort first, and afterwards the city, and then steal, rob, and carry away all the money and goods they could procure." The officer rushed the confession to one of the judges, signed with Peg's mark, to which the undersheriff attested. Pleased with himself, Horsmanden assumed that Peg was ready to reveal more in return for her life.

Caesar Varick and Prince Auboyneau had no such option. They were condemned to death for the burglary on May 8, and Justice Philipse read their sentences to them. But he was not done. He also defended the process through which they had been condemned. Unlike the slaves in the 1712 conspiracy and those slaves thought to have taken a part in the Stono rebellion, Caesar and Prince had been "proceeded against in the same manner as any white man." They had been indicted by a grand jury; permitted to call witnesses, cross-examine, and address the court; and had been found guilty by a jury "of twelve honest men upon their oaths." He failed to add that none of the men were African in origin, nor would any free black have been permitted to sit on the jury. This bar to a jury that included an African-American's peers continued well into the twentieth century in many Southern jurisdictions — until 1936, when the U.S. Supreme Court found that the systematic exclusion of people from a jury panel on the grounds of race was a violation of the Fourteenth Amendment.

Philipse insisted that he knew they had committed many more crimes, and that they were "very wicked fellows, hardened sinners, and ripe, as well as ready, for the most enormous and daring enterprises." There was no hope of reprieve, but if they earnestly prayed, they might be forgiven by a higher power. Only sincere repentance and confession of sin would save them from damnation. Philipse hoped that his hellfire-and-brimstone sermonette would frighten Caesar and Prince into revealing the full scope of the plot to burn down the city, but they remained mute.

The religious motif in Philipse's remarks was not mere convention. He believed that sin and crime went hand in hand, as did most of the white men in the courtroom that day. Christian beliefs clearly linked the two together. The irony was that the slaves were not Christians. Consequently, the admonition did not impress them as much as it did the jury. Perhaps Philipse realized that as well.

In fact, many Africans believed that their souls would leave their bodies at death and travel back to Africa, to live among the spirits of their ancestors in their homeland. Excavations of the Negro burial ground in New York City, just north of Wall Street, have revealed that when slaves were interred, African votive objects were placed in the coffins. Other religious objects have been found in excavations of slave quarters elsewhere in the colonies. Spiritual healers, priests, fortune-tellers, magicians, and suspected witches lived among the slaves in the New World, and no doubt New York City had its share. These men and women performed rites that combined Christian beliefs and African folk religious ideas. It is entirely possible that Caesar Varick and Prince Auboyneau may have welcomed the chance to lay down the burdens of slavery and join their ancestors. Slave suicide was not uncommon in the colonies, and two of the slaves who took part in the 1712 arson and murder plot killed themselves before they could be taken prisoner.

———

At some point in the inquiry, the arson plot had become a conspiracy to destroy the city and escape the bonds of slavery. Had it always been so and was it only now revealing itself, or did it grow in the minds of the prosecutors and from there find its way to the accused? The first source of information on what would later be termed the "Great Negro Conspiracy" was the newly penitent and suddenly voluble Peg. On May 8 and 9 she confessed to the court that she had spent time at Romme's dramshop and saw him incite "ten or eleven Negroes" with a plan to get rich. They would "burn the houses of them that have the most money, and kill them all." At the time Romme reminded all present of the 1712 uprising (but did not elaborate on the fate of those slaves) and insisted that the slaves gathered at his house must burn the fort first. Peg recalled that Cuffee Philipse liked the plan and urged the others to join in it, while Romme looked on approvingly. Peg named some of the attendees—Caesar Pintard, Cato Moore, Patrick English, Jack Breasted, Brash Jay, and Curaçao Dick (Dick being the forename, Curaçao the place of origin)—but none of these men had done anything more than listen. All but Cato, Curaçao Dick, and Caesar Pintard left soon thereafter. The remaining three slaves drank cider, played dice, and whispered among themselves. On other occasions Caesar Varick and Prince Auboyneau sat in.

By confessing to her attendance at Romme's, Peg was distancing herself and the conspiracy from Hughson's tavern. By pointing her finger at Romme, she was protecting her patron, Hughson. But by confessing to overhearing the plot she inadvertently put herself in the middle of a criminal conspiracy. According to colonial law, any white who abetted a slave conspiracy to incite rebellion was guilty of the offense whether or not the white did anything to further the objective of the conspiracy. In trying to gain leniency on the charge of receiving stolen goods—an offense for which courts often mitigated sentence—Peg had tightened the noose around her neck for the far more serious charge of abetting a slave uprising. Worse, the judges—knowing, as Peg did not, what Price had reported of their conversation in the jail—were not persuaded by her attempt to divert attention from Hughson.

Romme had fled, but his wife, Elizabeth, was summoned and examined. She denied any knowledge of criminal activity in her house but admitted that Caesar and Bastian Varick sometimes came by Romme's dramshop, as did Prince Auboyneau, Caesar Pintard, and Cato Moore. Peg, waiting in the wings, identified the slaves who were at Romme's nighttime assemblies. According to Horsmanden, one of them, Patrick English, had his guilt written all over his face and gave himself away with his gestures, so that the court instantly believed what Peg said of him. Mary Burton, shown the same gallery of slaves, denied that any of them except Caesar Varick, Cuffee, and Prince were familiar to her from Hughson's. Thus, Peg's confession was again confirmed. But she insisted that Hughson never engaged in anything like Romme's criminal activities. The court welcomed her revelations about Romme but still believed she knew more than she was saying about Hughson. She was therefore arraigned for the conspiracy along with John and Sarah Hughson, "upon the supposition that this step might probably be a means of bringing her to a resolution of making a full discovery of what she knew."

Peg's admissions, together with Burton's testimony, were probably enough to convict Cuffee and the other slaves on conspiracy charges since the court believed they had met at Hughson's tavern. That they went there to drink is very likely true. Did they also talk openly of fire, rape, and murder? Burton insisted they did, and her testimony was sufficient to commit them to jail. But Caesar and Prince had gone to the gallows without confessing their guilt, and without their confession, the entire prosecution might collapse. Certainly it would be much harder for the court to try the Hughsons and Peg for a part in a conspiracy that could just as easily have been limited to a few loudmouthed slaves.

The judges again turned to Price, putting him in a cell with Cuffee. Price was given the money to buy rum punch, which he shared with Cuffee. According to Price's deposition the next day, Cuffee admitted that he was a leader of the Geneva gang. He had nothing to do with the fires or the plot to burn down the city. Quaco Roosevelt had told him that he had set the fire at the fort. Quaco was a member of Smith's Fly Boys, and they were the culprits in the epidemic of fires. Thus, Cuffee Philipse followed Peg's lead in shifting the blame. Like her, he failed to realize that by admitting he took even a minimal part in a criminal conversation, he was legally guilty of conspiracy.

More important for the upcoming trial of John and Sarah Hughson for conspiracy, Cuffee placed Quaco at Hughson's tavern. Mary

Burton, when questioned about Quaco, testified that she had seen him at her master's place with the recently executed Prince and Caesar. Hughson had said, while in her presence, that he, his wife, and the slaves had all taken an oath on the Bible not to reveal to anyone the cause of the fires or the conversations about the killing of whites. Finally, Burton said she saw Caesar Varick give Hughson money to buy guns for the conspiracy.

The last statement was a bombshell. Most whites (Hughson apparently being the exception) feared nothing more than disgruntled slaves brandishing firearms. In 1680 the lawmakers of Virginia had addressed the issue directly: "Whereas the frequent meetings of considerable numbers of Negro slaves under pretense of feasts and burials is judged of dangerous consequence," slaves at such gatherings were not to carry firearms. Whenever a revolt was rumored in the West Indian colonies, the planters reminded one another to lock up their firearms. Although little in these hearings was made public, the news that slaves planned "to seize and carry away the arms" stored in the fort and "to seize their masters' arms," plus the fact that Hughson was rumored to have "bought and procured arms, ammunition, and powder for the purpose," was so shocking that it was reported in the *New-York Weekly Journal* on June 15, 1741. The fear had a solid grounding, for slaves had used firearms in the 1712 murders. In an abortive Virginia slave revolt in 1751, slaves armed themselves with muskets. Gabriel's rebellion in Richmond, Virginia, in 1800 featured a plan to seize the muskets in the city armory. In fact, evidence of Hughson's purchase of arms (which, however, never turned up) continued to accumulate in the court long after Hughson had rotted away in his chains. If one is to believe slave Adam Murray's confession, Hughson was said to have purchased the arms from a dancing master named Holt. The purchase of arms was a common theme in the slaves' testimony. This fact was never proven, but that did not attenuate the consequences. The court entertained all of these stories since there were no hard-and-fast rules excluding hearsay or rumor as evidence.

In the meantime, Cuffee Philipse and Quaco Walters languished in jail. Cuffee had become lachrymose and told everyone who would listen that he was doomed. Peg kept on confessing but only admitted to knowledge of stolen firkins of butter, gold coins, and cords of firewood that mysteriously appeared at Romme's door. The court knew better: Romme had fled after the Hogg robbery, and what Peg was describing had occurred not at Romme's but at Hughson's. The more she denied the involvement of the Hughsons, the more the court admonished her to the contrary. Yet she would not give them what they wanted. Her pardon was prepared, though not sealed. It would lie just outside her reach until she impeached John Hughson of his crimes.

The sad but potent truth anyone engaged in the study of modern criminal justice must concede is that everyone lies. It applies to the police on the witness stand as much as it does to the defendant and even the innocent witness. We lie because it is easier, because we wish to conceal, because the truth is embarrassing, or because we fear the repercussions that may follow from the truth. We lie to save ourselves, to blame others, to deny complicity of thought or deed. Peg lied. She may have been fond of the Hughsons or afraid of them, grateful to them or hoping to capitalize on her loyalty. She had seen Caesar, her lover and the father of her child, executed. She may have lied to protect his reputation or to spite those who had taken his life. A prostitute, she was a victim as well as a criminal. But she was also a woman who, in the face of adversity of the worst kind, had decided that the only control she had over her world was bound up with the words she chose to either utter or withhold from her prosecutors.

———

Peg's best efforts to save herself were undone by a bit player in the drama. Sandy (or Sawney) Niblet, a seventeen-year-old slave arrested for his suspected part in the conspiracy, was sweating out the weekend of May 15 in the city jail. Although he had little contact with the gangs and no one really trusted him, he nevertheless drank and gambled with their members. He was also the first slave to confess to the grand jury his personal knowledge of a plot. What he said was the ruin not only of his fellow slaves but of Peg and the Hughsons.

Sandy claimed to be a religious man. He had been taught by ministers to fear hell. He may have been a genuine convert to Christianity or, like his marginal attachment to the gangs, an off-and-on convert. He plainly feared authority of any kind yet loved being in the limelight. He told the grand jury that when Quaco Roosevelt asked him if he would join in a plot to torch the town, he said no, for he feared both hanging and damnation. But that did not prevent him from listening to the plotters. He overheard Quaco Walters and Cuffee Philipse plan to burn the Philipse warehouse; William, one of the Spanish prisoners of war, threaten mayhem if he were not returned to his "own country"; Curaçao Dick, Augustine, Anthony, and Juan — all Spanish Negroes — promise to set fires; Francis Bosch admit to setting fires; and Fortune Wilkins, Patrick English, and Cato Moore join in the plan to set fire to their master's houses. Was there any grand design behind all these threats? Sandy reported that, according to Quaco Roosevelt and Cuffee Philipse, "their design was to kill all the gentlemen, and take their wives."

The connection between an uprising and a mass rape may sound far-fetched, but rape was used as a tool by soldiers in wartime to crush the spirit of a defeated enemy. English officers in the eighteenth century attempted to curb the lascivious appetites of their men, but there was often a period of "havoc" after the successful assault of a besieged fortress or city. Rape of their masters' wives and daughters by slaves had even broader implications. Boasting of the day when the male slave could reverse the sexual superiority of whites would not have been unusual in any group like the carousers at Hughson's establishment. Slaves knew only too well that some white males abused their authority as masters or overseers to force sexual relations on female slaves. This conduct was illegal in New York — and probably far less common than it was in the slave South and the Caribbean — but fury at the prospect and impotence to prevent it bedeviled slave men. Imagining the freedom they would have to rape white women was one psychological device to divert their self-loathing and channel the anger some slaves experienced when they thought about the rape of black women by white men. Winthrop Jordan's brilliant retrieval of the conversations of slaves at Second Creek, Mississippi, at the beginning of the Civil War included much the same imagined inversion of sexual license that Quaco Roosevelt and Cuffee Philipse indulged. But it was also true that members of the two rival gangs that divided the city — the Long Beach Boys and Smith's Fly Boys — might simply have been engaging in one-upmanship, in a contest of sexual braggadocio.

In later years, courts hearing slaves' confessions (like Sandy's) would proceed with more caution — not out of respect for the slave but out of a deep conviction that a slave's confession could too easily be coerced and that slaves would say anything that came into their minds. Antebellum Southern judges like Raphael Semmes of Florida warned that "the almost absolute control which the owner has over the will of the slave, should induce the courts at all times to receive their confessions with the utmost caution and distrust." Confessions made under duress — for example, a slave threatened with bodily harm by officers of the law or a mob — or through the promise of favors ought equally to be suspect. Some of these courts (such as those in Georgia) ruled that all confessions made out of court should be excluded — an early form of the hearsay rule — though others (notably in Mississippi) turned a blind eye to evidence of coercion and ruled the confessions admissible. After all, was not coercion the foundation of all slavery? Why stop at coerced confessions?

The New York court wanted to hear the slaves' confessions and exhibited little caution about their admissibility. Instead, what made the trial of the slaves fair in the minds of the judges was what had made the slaves' confessions admissible in the first place, namely, the absolute conviction of the judges that they could distinguish truth from falsity. Thus, Horsmanden knew he could see through slave Patrick English's denials of complicity, for they were accompanied by a "fictitious hypocritical grin" and his "turning his eyes inward, as it were . . . their looks, at the same time, discovering all the symptoms of the most inveterate malice and resentment." But the slave Cork English's "cheerful, open, honest smile" spoke in his favor, though Cork had the inherited defect of "a countenance somewhat ill-favored, naturally of a suspicious look." Slaves' countenances supposedly betrayed their malice and their innocence, for black defendants in the dock could not control the tales their bodies told. The suspects might roll their eyes and throw up their hands, but the judges and jurymen could see past faces and gestures to the heart of the matter. Slave gestures constituted a kind of body language that masters could decipher at will. The slave who was lying made his body seem smaller, hunched his shoulders, shook, stuttered, and fluttered his hands. At least that was the common understanding of the master class.

———

By late May the number of suspected conspirators had grown from an intimate cadre of gang members to dozens of slaves whose ties to one another were informal and whose part in the conspiracy was unclear. Informants continued to add names; their information, often at second and third hand, led to more arrests. The entire slave community had come under scrutiny. On May 22 Fortune Wilkins followed Sandy Niblet to the grand jury room and told the jurors that a week before the fort went up in flames Quaco Roosevelt had tried to persuade him to scout out the fort, which Fortune claimed to have refused to do. A few days later Quaco pressed Fortune to join a band of arsonists, including Sandy Niblet and Cuffee Gomez. Rumor had it that Sandy, a frequent but inept arsonist, had tried to set fire to his master's house three times without success. Cuffee Philipse was part of the band, but Fortune said that he was not, nor did he ever lift a cup at Hughson's tavern. As a result of his testimony, three more slaves were committed to jail.

On May 25, not to be outdone by Fortune, Sandy told the grand jury that Fortune and Sarah Vanderspiegle had planned to set a fire in the market. He knew this because he had dropped in to a slave "frolick" at old man Comfort's house. There Sarah Burk, a female slave with considerable influence in gang circles, grabbed Sandy and threatened him if he did not drink with the others. Some of the slaves were whetting knives in the kitchen and threatened him as they asked, "Will you burn some houses?" Sandy, fearing for his life, promised that he would. Soon every male slave and a handful of women who worked in the city were at risk of being overheard or suspected of being present at one of these sessions.

The jurors and judges, assuming that a conspiracy of immense proportions existed, understandably credited those accounts which squared with their presuppositions. But the question remains: How big was this conspiracy? Although slaves pointed accusing fingers at one another, how seriously should one take their confessions? One cannot hear the slaves' voices. Moreover, can one trust the record itself? Laying aside deliberate mistakes and bias by the record keepers, the slaves' words might have been misheard or incorrectly recorded as a result of the hasty and frantic scribbling of clerks and sheriffs. There are two filters sorting the "facts" in the primary source records: the authorities' beliefs about what must have happened and the limitations of the record-keeping process itself.

How might these filters have colored the account that has come down to us? First, the jurors and judges might have heard only what they expected to hear. They assumed that slaves naturally inclined toward criminality or, alternatively, had loose morals and weak wills and thus could easily be led to commit crimes. They assumed that slaves could be made pawns of manipulative and unscrupulous whites like Hughson. Second, in their eagerness to get to the bottom of the matter and to identify all of the participants in the alleged conspiracy, the jurors, the prosecutors, and the judges who ran the examinations may have put words in the mouths of the witnesses. The most obvious instance of this was Clarke's April 17 offer of pardon and freedom to those who revealed the conspiracy. This applied to slaves who confessed their own complicity and would also be an inducement for those slaves who had grudges against other slaves or who wanted to be free and did not mind the opprobrium within the slave community resulting from naming conspirators. The latter might be guilty or innocent; the magistrates had no way of knowing for certain. It was the old problem of how to weigh the confessions of slaves.

The same inducement to confessors to name witches was a regular feature of English and European witchcraft trials and reemerged in the Salem witchcraft cases. Then, self-acknowledged witches swore that they had flown to black masses and met the devil — events that less panicky magistrates would not have credited (and, after 1693, did not credit). But the slaves who said what the judges wanted them to say in 1741 could put forth entirely plausible accounts of late-night oaths and plans to burn and kill whites.

Well aware of what the white power structure wanted to hear, some slaves may have repeated mere rumors as though they were fact or recast events they witnessed to make them appear more sinister and criminal. Slave informants' motives might have included the hope that a master would come to the defense of a pliant and helpful slave when his trial began, or that the court itself would show leniency. Indeed, in some cases the slaves might simply have tried to make themselves appear more important through their testimony—in effect turning the court into a stage and the slave into a self-conscious performer. The sameness of much of the testimony suggests that by the latter portion of the trials slaves knew exactly what they were supposed to say.

The judges' desire to get confessions and the confessors' desire to gain pardons may have widened the appearance of conspiracy far beyond its actual dimensions. One critic of the haste and bias of the Charleston freeholders' court that tried Vesey's supposed co-conspirators was William Johnson, a South Carolina lawyer and sitting Justice of the U.S. Supreme Court. In effect, as Michael Johnson has argued with respect to the Vesey case, the court would have created the conspiracy or at least distended its dimensions by inducing the confessors to swear that they had colluded with one another when, in fact, they had not. Loose and angry talk could easily be recast by the confessor or seen by the examiner as part of a real conspiracy. But Johnson did not deny that a conspiracy might have existed. He merely wanted the court to act like a proper criminal court. In the New York cases, the slave suspects were indicted by grand juries, were tried by petty juries, and had the right to speak in court and call their own witnesses. The Vesey defendants, including the free black Vesey himself, had none of these procedural rights. In the mental maps of the masters, slaves' unmonitored talk invariably led to insurrection. The masters agreed that it was better to nip a conspiracy in the bud, risking the punishment of the innocent, than to wake up to a conspiracy too late to prevent mayhem.

Some modern scholarly students of these trial records agree with the most paranoid of the judges and have turned the limited criminal conspiracy into a general uprising and the uprising into a lesson. For those historians who wish to glorify black resistance to slavery by means of these trials, there had to be a revolutionary cast to the conspiracy, and its object must have been freedom rather than theft or arson. Thus, some accounts of the 1741 events transform them into a revolt, an uprising, a rebellion, and an insurrection. The historians who propose these readings of trial records ironically accept the worst fears of the whites as well-grounded, with simple felons like Caesar becoming black versions of Spartacus, the Roman slave who led an uprising in the last century before the common era.

Both sides in this academic debate regard their position as one based on common sense. But it is a commonsense reading of documents that divides the two scholarly camps. Should the modern reader believe the slave who confesses to the plot, implicating hundreds, or the slave, facing the gallows, who persists in his innocence? Who had the most to lose by telling the truth? Who had the greatest reason to lie? In this controversy both sides are wont to forget that many slaves did not themselves know the truth. They may have heard it rumored that there was a plot (or multiple plots), or they may have overheard the plotters speak of their plans, but they had no way of determining if the plots were real or if the supposed plotters were telling the truth. Thus, they may have related to the authorities mere hearsay, which the magistrates, in their eagerness to uncover plots, treated as credible accounts.

Returning to the problem of correctly interpreting the slaves' testimony in the trial record, how much was put there by the auditors and how much by the recorder? To what degree did the slaves embroider their testimony to meet the expectations of their audience? How much were the slaves motivated by the hope of pardon? Many of the witnesses, including those most forthright in their confessions, seem to contradict one another on key points. Who was present at which meeting? Who said what? Who willingly took the lead, and who had to be persuaded at knifepoint?

One way to cut through this Gordian knot of conflicting testimony is to return to the concept of conspiracy. In some sense it does not matter who said what if the offense is conspiracy itself rather than treason. True, the law against conspiracy was a powerful prosecutorial weapon that left little scope for a strong defense, particularly when the defendants were slaves. To determine whether there was a conspiracy *in law* merely requires a yes or no answer to the following simple question: Did these individuals gather to discuss the commission of crimes? The answer undoubtedly is yes. So the problem for the historian is not to determine if there was a conspiracy but rather who was culpable of the charge.

Today one might argue that the New York colonial conspiracy statute was both vague and overly broad in its scope and definition. Indeed, it dealt to the prosecution all the high cards in the deck. Words constituted the conspiracy, but which words qualified? The prosecution decided and the jury would usually go along with its choice. The only question was: Did the defendant utter the words or merely listen to them? Even this did not really matter, for passive participation was still a crime. Specificity was not required either since any white master could be the target. The openness of the definition of the offense conferred immense discretion in an age when uncouth language and violent slang were part of the vernacular of working people. While strolling along the docks or visiting taverns in any city, one could hear violent and threatening oaths. Violence in domestic relations was equally common, and shrill threats of bodily harm routinely floated out the windows and doors of laborers' shanties into alleys and streets. Slaves beaten or verbally abused by their masters could not raise an arm or utter a curse in front of the assailant, so they aired their grievances in convocations of other slaves. Anyone in the company of slaves might have heard promises to kill someone or burn something down on any given day or night.

According to the court's reading of the law of conspiracy, just about every slave and many free blacks in the city and its environs might have been charged and — given the way the trial juries seemed to lean — convicted. Some of the principals who had been at Hughson's initial meeting, the "feast" the next day, or the drinking party (the "frolick") at Comfort's establishment later in the week must have mentioned the discussion to other slaves in the household or at work, if not actually pressing others to join. Were the listeners equally culpable? How about those present at Hughson's tavern who merely watched the proceedings but did not take part in the discussion or swear allegiance? The prosecution's definition of conspiracy implicated all of these men.

Slaves faced with these charges had few choices. One was how to plead. Did the plea of "not guilty" mean that the defendant had nothing to do with the conspiracy? Probably, but even those whose reported language was most vehement pleaded not guilty at first. Can the chorus of "not guilty" pleas be construed as proof that there was no conspiracy? Hardly. Remember how few slaves ever confessed to ordinary crimes. As the trials wore on, slave defendants switched from not guilty to guilty pleas. The fact that they all switched may indicate that those who were not guilty had decided to surrender and place themselves at the mercy of the court. They knew that no one would be acquitted. Were the confessions of the innocent so insincere as to be useless in proving the conspiracy? Hardly. Confessions simply meant that the suspects did not ask the prosecution to prove its case. Confessions, like not guilty pleas, were tactical moves in the cat-and-mouse game that all trials entail. For the slaves, the rules of the game were as unfair as slavery itself, yet they still had to abide by the rules.

———

On May 29 the first trial for the alleged rebels in the arson conspiracy began. Quaco Roosevelt and Cuffee Philipse were indicted for arson and for "wickedly, voluntarily, feloniously, and maliciously conspiring, combining and confederating with . . . diverse other Negroes to kill and murder the inhabitants of this city." Why two charges? Either would have been enough to execute the defendants. If one carefully examines the indictment, nothing required the prosecution to charge the two men with conspiracy to commit the crime *and* committing the crime. "Feloniously, and maliciously" were conventional elements in all indictments for serious offenses. Felony meant the charge was capital and malice (the intent to do harm) was an element of all felonies. "Wickedly" was boilerplate language; it proved that the criminal law was rooted in a common morality. Volition was another element of felony since the slaves could not aver that they had acted under duress or through a misunderstanding. So why indict for both crimes? The answer is both simple and disturbing: no one testified to actually seeing them set the fires. Evidence to support the charge of arson was only based on testimony concerning what the two men said before and after the fires. The fact that someone set fires in turn proved that two men had not spoken idly. The prosecution's case was circular, but the defendants could find no way out of the deadly circle.

Because he had no direct evidence that Quaco and Cuffee had set the fires, in his opening remarks for the prosecution Attorney General Bradley stressed both defendants' part in the conspiracy. He also knew that the conspiracy would worry the jury more than the fires. It was the conspiracy rather than the fires that riveted "the eyes of the inhabitants of this city and province" on the jury, for it was the conspiracy that imperiled "the future security and repose, that they may sit securely in their own houses, and rest quietly in their beds, on one daring to make them afraid." Bradley's opening remarks echoed the biblical promise of peace in Israel and Judah (1 Kings 4:25) on purpose. The slaves had brought the savagery of the jungle to the city. Only a Christian court imposing justice based on morality could restore harmony and order.

Horsmanden provided a fuller account of this slave trial than any other, for if Quaco Roosevelt and Cuffee Philipse could be convicted based solely on what they said, every other slave present at the nighttime meetings could either be convicted or made to turn state's evidence. These trials thus presaged much of what would follow. Mary Burton's testimony initiated the prosecution's case, and it was followed by that of other whites. Slave testimony came at the end. Burton said that Cuffee, Caesar, and Prince often met at Hughson's tavern and openly discussed plans to burn down the city. In these conversations Cuffee proved himself an amateur analyst of class structure: he felt that too few had too much, and soon his master — one of the richest men in the city — would have far less and Cuffee would have more. They planned to set the fires at night, and when the whites came to put them out, they would be killed — a replay of the 1712 attack.

It is possible that the slaves intended to reprise those events, but it is equally possible that Burton had heard about them and had used the story to embellish her own. According to her testimony, Cuffee had threatened her, claiming that when the insurrection was over she would become his wife. Hughson merely looked on and said nothing. Burton's admission of her fear of Cuffee and her anger at Hughson might provide sufficient motive for animosity toward them. If Cuffee had teased her and Hughson, her master, had not intervened, might she not have gained revenge against both through her accusations in court?

One might wish to know more about the men and women who stood in the dock and swore away the lives of the two defendants. (Court TV has spoiled us.) We cannot see their faces, hear the tone of their voices, or observe their gestures. Horsmanden did, and he recorded some of them, but we have already determined that his eye was jaundiced. For example, when Sarah Hughson Jr. refused to speak, she was described as "a miserable wretch," but when she became an accuser, Horsmanden found her face and voice "touched with visible marks and [the] semblance of sincerity and truth." He had nothing but contempt for the wily Bastian Varick until after he had confessed. Then Horsmanden recorded that Varick "seemed by his looks and behavior, upon his examination, to be touched with a remorse for his guilt. . . . Therefore it was judged proper to recommend him to the lieutenant governor for a pardon."

We are left with a recital of names and the bare bones of their testimony. Arthur Price confirmed that Cuffee had told him that Quaco Roosevelt set the fire at the fort, but Cuffee did not know how Quaco had accomplished the feat — nor did the court. Sarah Higgins averred that she had seen four Negroes next to Philipse's warehouse the day before it was set ablaze. Cuffee was one of them and "they shuffled about as though they would hide themselves." She returned with the watch, armed with swords, but the slaves had gone. Evidently witnesses who did not know the accused intimately had trouble telling one slave from another. John Peterson, who had worked for Philipse and knew Cuffee by sight, swore that he had seen him coming out of the door of the warehouse as it burned. Peterson said he had handed Cuffee a pail of water and had told him to pass it on. Peterson said he overheard Philipse, who had just arrived at the fire, deny that Cuffee could have come out of the building since he had just left him at work at the dock, but Peterson insisted that Philipse was mistaken. Jacob Stoudenburgh, who was also present that night, swore that Cuffee had leaped out of the warehouse window to escape the fire. He knew Cuffee well, but his account was diametrically opposed to Peterson's when it came to placing Cuffee at the scene. A good defense counsel would have made hay of the discrepancy between the two accounts, but Cuffee had no defense counsel. There were lawyers present — Smith and Murray, for starters — but they represented the crown as special counsel.

The next witness, Isaac Gardiner, had rushed to the fire at the fort and said he saw Cuffee there in the bucket brigade. Every time someone passed him a bucket he laughed and emptied its contents on the ground. Then he "hazzah'd, danced, whistled, and sang," acting the part of the addled slave. He and the other slaves pressed into service "made game" when cajoled to be more careful with the water. Daniel Gautier observed the fire on the roof of the fort chapel and doubted whether it could have been caused by an over-turned plumber's firepot. The master plumber, one Hilliard, denied that he had caused the fire, for he had been very careful and even had a soldier with him as an aid. His firepot had a lid, and he kept the lid on when the firepot was not needed.

Fortune Wilkins and Sandy Niblet, the slaves who had confessed to overhearing the conspiracy, were called up. They had been waiting in the jail. Would they be charged? Their concern made them perfect witnesses against Cuffee and Quaco. Although they had not seen Cuffee or Quaco set any fires, their words ensured the convictions of Cuffee and Quaco. Fortune told the court that he had seen Cuffee on his way to the warehouse, along with two of the Spanish slaves. Fortune had gone with Quaco to the fort, entering the kitchen by a back route. A few days later, outside the fort, Quaco met Fortune again and dismissed Fortune's fear of being caught by the soldiers on watch. Two days before the fire Quaco had told Fortune that the fort was to be burned down. The day after the fire, Sandy Niblet told Fortune that "we have done the business," to which Quaco, present at the meeting, jokingly replied, "Don't you remember I told you there would be great alterations at the fort?" At that time Quaco admitted that he, Sandy, and Cuffee Gomez had set the fire. But Sandy, who was standing nearby, denied that he had set any fires. Now called to testify, he said that Quaco had torched the fort.

The prosecution needed to convince the jury that the defendants had the motive as well as the opportunity and the ability to cause the offense. In Cuffee's and Quaco's cases, the motive for the fires was established by their part in the conspiracy. That is why the prosecution worked so hard to place them at Hughson's tavern when the talk turned to firing the city. No one believed that Cuffee and Quaco were obedient, dutiful, law-abiding servants. Opportunity—

those unaccountable few minutes away from their tasks on the days in question — was there as well. Causation — hot coals in the warehouse fire; the absence of other possible causes in the fort conflagration — could be inferred by the jury.

In their defense, Cuffee and Quaco summoned their masters. It was not childlike dependency that led the slaves to ask for their masters' assistance — they needed alibis. Philipse swore that Cuffee was working on a boat shortly before the fire at the warehouse was discovered. Roosevelt testified that Quaco was cutting ice in the yard the entire morning that the fire occurred at the fort. James McDonald, the sentry at the fort's gate the day of the fire, testified that he had threatened to club Quaco to keep him out of the fort but could not since Quaco insisted on seeing his wife in its kitchen. But McDonald could not place Quaco on the roof of the fort, where the fire purportedly began. Other than their adamant denials, Quaco and Cuffee offered no further defense. They were not able to provide an airtight alibi for the times when the fires were set, nor would their masters give them "good character."

When the slaves had completed their defense, Smith summarized the prosecution's case for the jury. He surely knew that he had won. The jury knew all about the fires and, in fact, probably were acquainted with Cuffee and Quaco as well. The modern requirement that a jury not only remain impartial and have no contact with the parties involved but also that pretrial publicity not unduly influence a jury was unheard of in eighteenth-century colonial trials. It would have been virtually impossible to find a jury that did not know about the fires, the rumored slave uprising, the nighttime meetings at Hughson's and Comfort's establishments, and the identities of the various principals in the affair. Smith admitted as much in his opening remarks: "that a most horrid conspiracy has been formed, to burn this city, and to destroy the white people."

From the outset Smith played the eighteenth-century version of what today is called "the race card." His fiery racism further inflamed the all-white jury's existing prejudices. He ridiculed the presumption of slaves to titles like "governor," and in the next breath condemned the "monstrous" plot to make white women "prey to the rapacious lust of these villains." The "folly" and the "wickedness" of the defendants were shared by all the men of their race, who would soon stand where Quaco and Cuffee stood. Men like them were "heathen" and "pagan." The whole course of the matter proved "the monstrous ingratitude of this black tribe. Their slavery among us is generally softened with great indulgence; they live without care, and are commonly better fed and clothed, and put to less labour, than the poor of most Christian countries." Why were they not loyal and dutiful? The law protected them for "none can hurt them with impunity." Why did they persistently violate the law? The answer lay in their natures. They were a "brutish and bloody species of mankind." Only constant watchfulness of slaves by their masters would avert future plots.

Smith could have gained a conviction on the evidence as presented, particularly with the jury he had, but he knew that more trials were to come. In effect, he was telling the jury that their verdict in this case would enable the court to proceed with far less well documented cases against slaves and their white confederates to come, cases in which no overt act was involved or could be proven. He insisted "that great numbers of persons have been concerned in the plot, some whites, and many blacks." They must be ready for the trial of John Hughson, "captain of this hellish band."

At the same time that he excoriated the slaves and all Africans, he defended the government. His version of the plot, so hellish on its face, was cartoonlike as well: "Had it not been in part executed before it was discovered, we should with great difficulty have been persuaded to believe it possible that such . . . a foolish plot could be contrived by any creatures in human shape." The jury, the audience at the trials, and the citizens of the city could indeed sleep peacefully in their beds. Their government would protect them and their property — but only if the jury did its duty and convicted the defendants. The jury withdrew, "and being soon returned, found the prisoners guilty of both indictments."

From the bench Horsmanden immediately delivered sentence. As he recalled it years later his rhetoric was as impassioned as Smith's. Surely his purpose was identical, namely, to demonstrate the inherent immorality of the slave, "ye, and the rest of your color." God saw their wickedness, and God would punish it in the world to come. For the present, those humane and considerate masters — here Horsmanden addressed not the defendants or the jury but the public — "having given you the opportunities of forming this villainous and detestable conspiracy," must now prepare themselves for the discovery of their slaves' "vices, treachery, blood-thirstiness, and ingratitude." Turning to the defendants once again, he demanded: "Ye must confess your whole guilt . . . ye must discover the whole scene of iniquity which has been contrived in this monstrous confederacy, the chief authors and actors." Only when their credulous masters had absorbed the lesson of the malicious slaves' confession of the full extent of the plot would all whites be safe.

Both Quaco and Cuffee were to be burned at the stake. At the execution site, perhaps hoping against hope that a last-minute confession would bring a reprieve — Horsmanden thought they might be so inclined — Cuffee and Quaco broke their silence. Quaco confessed to his master, who was standing nearby, that Hughson was the author of the plot. He had enlisted Caesar Varick, Prince Auboyneau, Cuffee Philipse, and other slaves in the Geneva gang to burn the houses, rob the inhabitants, and bring the stolen goods to his tavern. On this point Mary Burton had told the truth. Quaco had started the fire at the fort, and Cuffee had done the same at the warehouse. Quaco's wife was innocent, as was the lieutenant governor's boy, Denby, and the slave fiddler Jamaica Ellis. Finally, he forgave McDonald for not admitting him to the fort.

Cuffee deposed to George Moore, the deputy secretary of the colony, who officiated at the execution site, that Hughson was indeed the lead conspirator, that Sandy Niblet was one of the incendiaries, along with Cuffee Gomez, and that he, Cuffee Philipse, had set the fire in his master's warehouse by running from the boatyard while carrying a lighted coal placed inside two clam shells in his pocket. In all, roughly fifty slaves were involved. He agreed to tell more if he were permitted to live a little longer.

His last words were drowned out by the crowd. Sensing that Moore might untie Cuffee and return him to the city hall to continue his confession, the crowd surged forward. They had gathered at the execution ground on the outskirts of the city to witness the immolation of the two slaves, and they were determined that the execution take place. Moore sent the sheriff to ask the lieutenant governor for an order to remove both men from the stakes. Even if he could have persuaded the crowd that the confessions were more important than the executions, Moore was not going to make this decision on his own. He finally left the grounds and rushed to the lieutenant governor's mansion, but the sheriff intercepted him and told him that without troops no one could rescue the convicts. That day's events concluded with the burning of Cuffee and Quaco.

Their deaths did not put an end to the trials. Indeed, based on their eleventh-hour confessions, seven more slaves were added to the dozen already in custody. Although the preliminary trials of the conspirators were over, the tribulations of their purported followers had only just begun.

CHAPTER 6

The "Great Negro Conspiracy"

The May trials had all involved defendants in patently criminal activities: burglary, theft, receiving stolen goods, and arson. From June 1 through the middle of July the court focused on the conspiracy itself. The conviction of the arsonists had confirmed the existence of a conspiracy. The court now had to discover the identity of everyone involved. In the rush to judgment some innocent parties might be convicted, but that did not particularly trouble the authorities. The conspiracy itself was so dangerous to the state that every means must be utilized to quash it. And those innocent men had probably committed other crimes that they had hidden. As Justice Frederick Philipse had already told Caesar Varick and Prince Auboyneau, he was certain that they were "wicked" men who had gotten away with crime previously.

Most of the evidence of criminal conversations among slaves came from slaves who attended the various meetings of the supposed conspirators. Although there is no evidence that slaves were physically tortured to produce confessions, the prospect of ending like Caesar and Prince certainly motivated slaves to testify against one another. At the beginning of June Sandy Niblet returned to court to be examined by Horsmanden. He revealed himself an able eavesdropper. Evidently he had a good deal of time on his hands — ironically, both Horsmanden and Smith had pointed to idleness as one of the root causes of the slaves' criminal activity — and spent it lurking in shadows and standing by open doors and windows to listen to conversations among conspirators.

Each time he returned to court, he revealed a little more about the meetings. Like Mary Burton, he had something of the tease in him. At the Comfort house "frolick," for example, he recalled, Jack Comfort and Sarah Burk had occupied themselves sharpening pen-knives. As he worked at the whetstone, Jack also talked about killing all the white men and having "all the wives for themselves." Sandy also revealed a good memory for faces. At Comfort's place he saw Cato Moore, Caesar Pintard, Brash Jay, Dundee Todd, Robin Chambers, Patrick English, Caesar Peck, Cato Cowley, Cook Comfort, Harry Kipp, Tom Moore, Pompey Leffert, Prince Duane, Caesar Varick, three unnamed country "Negroes," and Mr. Comfort's "old Coromantee woman." Proud of himself, Sandy added, "the room being quite full." He was also hanging about when Fortune Wilkins discussed the burning of the fort with Augustine a week before the event took place. As a result of his rambling but remarkably detailed accusations, Tom Moore, Prince Duane, and Pompey Leffert were arrested.

Sandy had good reason to embellish his testimony, for he was more than a mere hanger-on, having agreed to join in the conspiracy. Fortune Wilkins told Horsmanden that "Niblet's boy" was relaying messages between groups. According to Fortune, Sandy not only overheard the details of the plot but was knee-deep in the planning.

———

Sarah Burk, who also put Sandy close to the center of events, was the only female slave to testify. In conversation with Judge Philipse and John Chambers, she admitted that she had been present that Sunday afternoon at Comfort's house. She had threatened to eject Sandy if he did not drink. She was tired of his mooching off everyone and considered him a lazy young lout. He annoyed her — and probably everyone else. But his pesky presence was not the revelation in Sarah's account. Sarah identified the female slaves who were present at the meetings. They did not make threats or promise to commit crimes, but Sarah Teller, Betty Clopper, and Jenny Hunt were all associates of the Long Beach Boys, who had sworn to carry out the plot. The women made supportive noises, but they were quiet when the men talked about carrying off the wives of their masters.

When her testimony was read back to her, Sarah Burk "retracted" a portion of it and "excused many persons." Although Horsmanden noted the latter, he did not notice that all the women were now "excused." He was vexed by the recantation and, worse, by Sarah's demeanor. She "was one of the oddest animals among the black confederates, and gave the most trouble in her examinations. A creature of an outrageous spirit." When examined, she "threw herself into the most violent agitations, foamed at the mouth, and uttered the bitterest imprecations." No wonder Sandy did what Sarah Burk told him to do. But above all she protected the other slave women by promising to tell all and then recanting what she said. A clever, strong, and compelling person, she was the slaves' confidante and, in the end, confided little to the court.

There is no doubt that slave women laid the tables, prepared the food, and joined in the dancing and singing at the "frolicks." Nevertheless, as historians Philip D. Morgan and George D. Terry report concerning one rumored rebellion in South Carolina, "men seem to have dominated the various dancing and drinking sessions referred to in a number of independent slave testimonies." Women might be "fabricators" of stories about men, but rebellion was a man's work. The division of labor in general was a characteristic of colonial "domestic economy." Women and men most often worked in the company of others of their sex. Here it applied to conspiracy. The same pattern appeared in other North American slave rebellions. In Gabriel's rebellion, according to historian James Sidbury, "the world described during the insurrection trials was overwhelmingly male . . . which may explain why Black men did not include women in their plans for violent rebellion." Although much of the plotting for that 1800 revolt took place "at barbeques . . . not one witness to these events described an incident in which men and women did anything together."

The women present at the Comfort house were probably members of that household, neighbors, women friends of the men, and (in modern terms) "affiliates" of the two gangs, but they do not seem to have included any of the men's wives. As we have seen, the law did not aid or protect the formation of slave families. Despite Burk's recantation, the drinking party at Comfort's place no doubt included women. Of primary interest is not her recantation but rather the fact that none of the men mentioned women except Sandy, and the only woman he mentioned was Burk. Later confessions by Jack Comfort and others similarly omitted the names of the women. For some of the men, apparently, the women were not important enough to include, but other men were obviously protecting their women from prosecution.

In the end, slave women were almost entirely absent from the indictments. Only Sarah Burk was arraigned on an indictment. She confessed to her presence at the meeting and was reprieved and sold to a buyer in Hispaniola. Cuba (who belonged to Mrs. Lynch), Sarah Depeyster, and Sarah Niblet were sent to jail but not indicted. The pattern again resembled that of other real or imagined revolts. In Gabriel's rebellion not one woman was indicted. In the wake of Nat Turner's 1831 rebellion in Virginia, only one woman was numbered among the forty-nine slaves brought to trial.

It may be that slave women's relative immunity was due to their owners' needs. White widows often owned slaves: Mrs. Burk owned Sarah, the widow Van Rantz owned York, and Mrs. Bickley owned Robin. Only Mrs. Kipp's Harry lost his life to the hangman. The three Spanish Negroes that Mrs. Carpenter and Sarah Maynard owned jointly were sold to the Spanish West Indies after they had been convicted. Mrs. Kierstede's Braveboy and Mrs. Ellison's Billy were arraigned but not convicted. Mrs. Fortune's Cuffee confessed and was sold to a master in Surinam. Slave families were of little importance in this world.

———

The Hughsons now returned to center stage to be tried for their role in the conspiracy. On June 2 John, his wife Sarah, his daughter Sarah, and Peg were arraigned on a new indictment for abetting and encouraging the arson plot. The pursuit of the mother and daughter were meant to induce Hughson to confess his role in the affair, but he denied everything when the court refused to offer him a pardon in return for his confession. Trial upon all the indictments was set for June 4.

Throughout these proceedings the role of the two Sarahs remained problematic. In the end their fates were entirely different, with the narrative explaining some — but not all — of the reasons for this distinction. The English common law that New York received from England made Sarah Sr. a subordinate partner in John's life. The doctrine was called "femme covert," a term derived from Law French (a singular and awkward combination of English,

French, and Latin gracing law treatises and reports in the fifteenth and sixteenth centuries). By the middle of the eighteenth century the law of England was written in English, but Law French survived in the dusty corners of technical law. Still, "femme covert" was anything but a relic of a bygone age. It dictated that after marriage the wife's identity merged with her husband's. Her property (save that which she inherited after the marriage) was his to do with as he chose. She could not dispose of it without his permission. The children were his, not hers, and she could only divorce him if he abandoned her for seven years or committed a felony. She could not execute a contract without his signature or consent, but he did not need hers. The flip side of this legal debility of married women is that they could argue that they were not legally liable for the crimes their husbands committed even if they were proven to be accessories. The logic of the plea was that they had no choice in the matter. As married women acting under the orders of their husbands, they had no volition in the eyes of the law.

Sarah Jr. did not have this excuse, but had she been a minor she might have claimed diminished responsibility. Modern law makes exceptions for minors' culpability in criminal activities. At the very least the prosecution must obtain the permission of the court to try a minor as an adult. In many states those minors under sixteen years of age cannot be tried as adults. A recent increase in gang-related homicides, where minors were chosen to commit crimes precisely because state law protected them from being tried as adults, has resulted in a blurring of age distinctions in law. In early-modern England and its colonies, there was never an automatic exemption for children in their teens. They could be tried on capital charges if the prosecution desired, though often judges and juries would ask leniency for them and pardons were common. At the same time, English law did not regard a small child as fully capable of knowing the difference between right and wrong. Sarah Jr. was described as a "single woman" in the court records. She was old enough to be responsible for her actions, but as the trial wore on the court could see that she was still under the thumb of her father.

John Hughson began his trial defense in the same tone as he used to the grand jury. He was confident — even arrogant — and conceded nothing. He challenged — as was his right — sixteen of the twenty jurors allowed him by law and also insisted on exercising the peremptory challenges his wife and daughter were permitted. A man used to commanding his little fiefdom, he could not have appeared a sympathetic figure in the dock. The charges were read — namely, that John, Sarah Sr. and Jr., and Peg had conspired with Caesar Varick, Prince Auboyneau, and Cuffee Philipse to set the fires and kill the town's "inhabitants." The grand jury (in the language of the indictment) did not include slaves or free blacks among the "inhabitants," for the supposed plot only referred to whites. The blacks, representing some 18 percent of the city, were invisible for the moment.

The prosecution had to prove that the Hughsons and Peg were a party to the conspiracy rather than mere bystanders. That is, the Hughsons were not just present but jointly with Peg had administered the oath of loyalty and silence to the slaves. Having convicted Caesar, Prince, and Cuffee by suggesting that they were behind the plot, Attorney General Bradley now reversed his field and proposed that it had all been Hughson's idea. Supposedly he had advised, encouraged, and assembled the slaves; given them drink; and initiated the oaths. He had agreed to buy guns and ammunition to arm the slaves. He was a monster.

Why all this bother? Although Hughson was already convicted of a felony whose punishment could be death, his crime of receiving stolen goods might not be enough to condemn him. In fact, conviction on a charge of receiving stolen goods usually did not lead to the gallows. The prosecution needed a conviction on the conspiracy charge to execute Hughson. Moreover, the attorney general wanted him to confess. If he did, it would prove that the apparatus of criminal justice in the colony, already suspect for overlooking the plot, was now up to speed. Hughson's conviction and confession would exonerate the court and the lieutenant governor from the charge of failure to protect the public weal. For the present, Bradley had to content himself with a succession of demonstrative accusations: "This is that Hughson! Whose name and most detestable conspiracies will no doubt be had in everlasting remembrance, to his eternal reproach. . . . This is the man! That great incendiary! That arch rebel against God, his king, and his country. That devil incarnate, and chief agent to the old Abaddon of the infernal pit, and Geryon [a three-headed monster from ancient Greek mythology] of darkness." How one could be the devil and his agent at one and the same time did not concern Bradley. To make sure that Hughson did not get away on this occasion — he had slipped through the crown's fingers on previous charges — the court named William Smith, Joseph Murray, James Alexander, and John Chambers, the illuminati of the New York City bar, as special prosecutors. One has to wonder if the court acted to preempt Hughson from retaining one of the four for his defense.

———

The references that Bradley and Horsmanden made to the irreligion of Hughson and the slaves may seem like more boilerplate, since every indictment for a capital offense included the phrase "without the sight of God before his eyes" or some similar formula. But here the invocation of the wrath of God meant more. The crown had enjoined ministers and missionaries in the colony to convert the Indians and the slaves to Christianity so that they might be more docile and loyal to their masters. More important, in the years immediately preceding 1741 numerous slaves in New York City had seemed ready to convert. In 1739 the evangelical itinerant preacher George Whitefield arrived in the city. He was one of the foremost of the so-called Great Awakening ministers, calling on his listeners to confess their sins and seek salvation. The charismatic Anglican divine addressed thousands in the city. On November 26, 1739, the *New-York Weekly Journal* reported that "his discourses were pathetic and tinctured with charity. He had audiences more numerous than is seen on such occasions, for it has been observed that there were more on the outside of the meeting house wall than within."

Whitefield's message was one of self-examination and confession of sin. Those who attended his sermons most often came away deeply moved: "With what a flow of words, what a ready profusion of language . . . he looked as if he was clothed with authority from the Great God." Whitefield was not happy with the way that slaveholders treated their bondsmen, and he said so publicly in 1740: "Think you, your children are in any way better by nature than the poor negroes? No! In no wise! Blacks are just as much, and no more, conceived and born in sin, as white men are; and both if born and bred up here, I am persuaded, are naturally capable of the same improvement." Whitefield did not call for the abolition of slavery — he had defended it in England — but rather demanded that slaves be treated decently. He went even further: "Although I pray God the slaves may never be permitted to get the upper hand, yet should such a thing be permitted by Providence, all good men must acknowledge the judgment would be just."

The connection between Whitefield's condemnation of slavery and the slaves' plan to free themselves seemed obvious. One of the accused conspirators even blamed Whitefield: "It was through the great encouragement the Negroes had from Mr. Whitefield we had all the disturbance." Horsmanden railed against "suspicious vagrant strolling preachers" who convinced slaves that their crimes were righteous acts and would be rewarded in the next world. Such incautious preaching "raised up a bitter spirit in the Negroes against their masters."

———

If Hughson's and his confederates' crimes seemed proof that both he and the slaves did not understand the true message of Christianity — he had misused the Bible; they had violated the biblical injunction to slaves to be obedient — there was another reason for the vigorous prosecution of Hughson and his family: the court was sending a message to the white population of the colony. Despite the legal prohibitions dating from 1712 through 1731 against serving alcohol to slaves, harboring runaways, and entertaining slaves after the curfew, many whites at all levels of society were guilty of these things. Motivated by profit or benevolence, whether committed on purpose or through negligence, whites violated the law. The common council took note of the violations, but since its members were no doubt also guilty (who would not allow a trusted house slave to entertain a friend in the kitchen after hours?), and nothing came of the violations, they were not prosecuted. A partial mutuality, a kind of civility, had developed over time between whites and blacks that ran athwart the letter of the law. Using Hughson's case the colonial government warned that what masters did not know about slaves' conversations in their own houses could lead to the destruction of the colony.

The prosecution read the accusations of Cuffee Philipse and Quaco Roosevelt into the record against Hughson. Even though these confessions were made at the stake in hope of a reprieve, the court admitted them. Hughson had an opportunity to cross-examine Undersecretary Moore and Mr. Roosevelt. A clever counsel could have used this opportunity to challenge the truth of the confessions by working backward and pointing to the efforts of Moore to prevent the executions. (A direct challenge to the confessions as more prejudicial than probative would have required the law of evidence to be far more sophisticated than it was at the time.) Hughson let the opportunity pass.

Burton and various soldiers from the fort who drank at Hughson's tavern testified that the slaves gathered there regularly and that the family joined in the drunken oath-taking using the household Bible. At this the defendants' seeming indifference vanished. They began hugging one another and crying out that they were good parents. Hughson kissed his daughter and Sarah Sr. called for their youngest child, whom she held to her breast. The judges ordered an end to the theatrical display of family affection. Indeed, Horsmanden's account of this episode bordered on the snide. He opined that the dramatic gestures were meant to "move compassion in the judges and jury," but Hughson would have been better advised to orchestrate such a cynical playlet long before this moment. A more likely scenario is that Hughson and his wife had realized the full import of their role in the conspiracy trials. They would not be reprieved because their conviction on the conspiracy charges was necessary to frighten the whites in the community. Had the court merely wanted their contrition and the names of the slaves who were present at their table, they might have engineered a last-minute commutation. As it was, their fate was sealed.

Recovering himself, Hughson spat back in defiance. If he was to die, he would tell the prosecution witnesses what he thought of them. Burton was a turncoat and the others were unworthy of a reply. In his defense Hughson called his neighbors as witnesses. They swore that they had seen nothing amiss in his business. In particular, Gerardus Comfort, at whose house Sarah Burk presided, saw "no harm" in the slaves who frequented Hughson's tavern. After all, they congregated in his kitchen as well. Hughson must have known that the jury would return a guilty verdict. When his time came to address the jury, he declared his complete innocence, as did his wife, daughter, and Peg. Had he assumed the entire blame, he might have saved them, but he was a bully as well as a thug and they said not a word.

In his summation for the prosecution, William Smith was more fulsome. Hell would be Hughson's lot. Smith even accused Hughson of "plunging himself and his family" into the pit of the inferno. One supposes that Smith's purpose was to show that Hughson was an evil husband and father, undercutting any sympathy the jury might have retained from the hugging episode earlier in the trial, but from a logical standpoint Smith's digression into domestic homily was a misstep. If Hughson had forced his family into committing a crime, how could they be blamed? Might they not have taken oaths out of fear of him and his demonic slave minions? As wife and daughter, did they have the requisite intent, as a matter of law, to be considered guilty of the offense?

From the bench Horsmanden tried to repair any damage that Smith's illogic may have caused the prosecution's case. Horsmanden instructed the jury that if they did not believe the witnesses for the crown, they must acquit, but if they found the prosecution witnesses credible, they must convict. He intentionally avoided mentioning the problem of whether the two Sarahs were culpable, perhaps hoping that the sword still hanging above their heads would persuade Hughson to confess. The jury was given the weekend to ponder its verdict, as was Hughson, who must have realized that all his wife and child needed to live was his willingness to accept his own fate. On Monday, June 8, the court reconvened and the guilty verdict was read to the four defendants. Justice Philipse told them that their real crime was "to be guilty not only of making Negroes their equals, but even their superiors, by waiting upon, keeping with, and entertaining them with meat, drink, and lodging."

If any of the whites in the packed courtroom had missed the implications of Smith's address to the jury, Philipse's sentencing address hammered home the message: there could be no social order if the two races commingled on anything like equal terms; that would only lead to "disorders, confusion, desolation, and havoc." For John and

Sarah Sr., Philipse had a special message: "Look upon your poor unhappy daughter . . . consider and set her a good example." In other words, confess before it was too late to save your souls.

Hughson was not the only male member of his family suspected of treating blacks as equals. His father, Thomas, and his four brothers — Nathaniel, Walter, William, and Richard — were also deemed to have blurred the color line. At least that is the only charge that the record hints could be laid at their feet. They would be arrested a week later, languish in jail until September 24, and finally be pardoned on condition that they leave the colony. John Hughson's trial was, if nothing else, a lesson to his clan that the government's interest included not only the prosecution of crime but also enforcing the subordination of one race to another.

———

Monday, June 8, was a busy day in court. The judges not only pronounced their sentence on the Hughsons and Peg but they ordered the trial of the next six slaves accused in the conspiracy. These trials — necessary to "expose" the lingering danger and make "examples" of all who joined in the plotting — were the closest thing to police state trials. Their purpose was not just to punish criminal acts or plots but to prevent thoughts of insurrection from even being verbalized. That is the way in which a tyranny guards itself against dissenters. The defendants had attended the sessions at Hughson's and Comfort's establishments. There they put into words their anger at their continuing oppression. They would rape and burn and kill. They would destroy the colony. They would take the government into their own hands.

To digress briefly, on its face the Zenger case seems to have little or no relationship to slave conspiracies, but Zenger's offense had also been mere words. This was not unusual in eighteenth-century criminal law. In England and its colonies criticism of the crown was always a criminal offense under the rubric "seditious libel." In many of the colonies, using the name of God in vain was considered a crime of blasphemy. Moreover, it was far easier to obtain evidence of words than of deeds. Zenger was acquitted because he had powerful friends and an able counsel. The slaves had neither.

On June 12, Jack and Cook Comfort, Caesar Peck, Cuffee Gomez,

Robin Chambers, and Jamaica Ellison stood trial upon the indictment for conspiracy. Quaco Roosevelt's and Cuffee Philipse's confessions were read to the jury, and Sandy Niblet and Sarah Burk testified, as they had to the grand jury. Whoever was at the meeting and expressed general assent to the remarks of the most virulent protesters was liable to the charge. The "most forward" of the slaves had to be punished as an example.

The defendants did not know what to ask because they did not know what constituted the legal elements of a defense. As Horsmanden reported, they asked "a few trifling questions." He did not even bother to enter these into the record, so we have no way of knowing what the defendants were thinking. The judges in English courts sometimes helped defendants frame their questions in the absence of defense counsel. Here the judges did the opposite. They were, for all intents and purposes, part of the prosecution. In the record, as in the courtroom, the defendants become mere names in a growing list of those slaves of whom an example was to be made. There was no effort to distinguish among the six or to allow them separate defenses. In the court, as in the law, they had no personality or individuality. After "a short stay" the jury returned and pronounced a guilty verdict. All were to be burned at the stake save Jamaica Ellison, who was to be hanged. They were all scheduled to die the next day.

But the court was not finished with its business. Bastian Wilkins, Francis Bosch, Albany, and Curaçao Dick were led into the court, arraigned on the indictment for conspiracy, and pleaded not guilty. Their trial would begin the next day. The wheels of justice were turning at full speed. As William Smith Jr., a lawyer himself, wrote many years after the events occurred, "A coincidence of slight circumstances, was magnified by a general terror into violent presumptions, tales collected without doors, mingling with the proofs given at the bar, poisoned the minds of the jurors." What Smith did not say was that his father, William Smith Sr., was the most virulent of the special prosecutors. In effect, the son was apologizing for the father's errant enthusiasm. But one had to be there to realize that "there was no resisting the torrent of jealousy, when every man thought himself in danger from a foe in his own house. The infection seized the whole legislature and . . . the grand jurors." One should note that William Smith Jr. also had a special perspective his father lacked: two years before he wrote his account of these events, the son had been driven from his home by a violent revolutionary mob and had witnessed persecution of loyalists based on equally flimsy circumstantial evidence.

As the June sessions continued, more of the accused slaves dove through the escape hatch that Sandy and Fortune Wilkins had opened by turning informer. Jack Comfort was the next to follow that course. From his and the others' testimony about him one gets the picture of a conniver who liked to be where the action was. Horsmanden called him a "crafty, subtle fellow" well suited to "corrupting other slaves," as though he was a known quantity to the judges. In fact, they depended on hearsay, for Horsmanden conceded that "his dialect was so perfectly Negro and unintelligible, it was thought it would be impossible to make any thing of him without the help of an interpreter." No one asked if he needed this service or offered it to him when he was to defend himself in court, but now an interpreter was found. One of Comfort's sons had worked with Jack in the cooper's trade and knew enough of his patois to serve as his interpreter.

Most of the slaves in New York had spent some time in the West Indies and either spoke English, a creole tongue, or at least a pidgin. From its inception slavery presented a communication problem since the West African languages spoken by the slaves had little in common with European languages. It was an old problem for peoples who encountered one another. Jack's examination took three days, in part because his testimony had to be translated for the inquisitors and their questions had to be translated for him. Only then could his revelations be recorded. When he was done, nine more slaves were apprehended, and his execution was delayed — permanently, as it turned out, for he received a pardon from the lieutenant governor upon application from the judges.

Jack told Chief Justice James DeLancey, who had just returned from a trip to Boston, about the role of the Spanish Negroes in the plot. Their participation, according to him, was crucial to the enterprise because they had gained fighting experience while serving in the Spanish fleet. In fact, they assumed that the Spanish would soon assault the port. Six of these men — Wan, Albany, Anthony, and three others — along with Quash Rutgers, Bastian Wilkins, and Ben Marshall, whose tales of the Spanish Negroes' prowess had first kindled Jack's interest, gathered at Hughson's tavern. There they ate fowl, mutton, bread, and drank punch. Peg, Sarah Sr. and her daughter, and Hughson sat on one side of the table, with the slaves on the other, as Hughson asked Ben "who would be the head man or captain for to rise?" Then the slaves began to boast about how many whites they would kill. Quash said he would kill five. York Marschalk would kill his mistress, who had scolded him. The others — including London Marschalk, Scipio Van Borsom, Cato Shurmur, and Cato Provoost — promised to set their masters' houses on fire. The Spanish Negroes also spoke, but Jack could not understand them.

Jack said that Curaçao Dick had arrived late at the feast but took the lead in making everyone swear to perform the deed. With much cursing and muttering, the Spanish Negroes agreed (though how anyone knew what they were saying was never explained). Other latecomers, seeking a bit of mutton or a piece of poultry, agreed to join. Tickle Carpenter, Bastian, Francis Bosch, and Cook Comfort nodded their assent, presumably with their mouths full. Jonneau Varick hesitated at the door until the meat was served, then entered and began to eat. The price of admission was joining the conspiracy, which he did.

Jack continued: the same crew — minus the Hughsons, Burton, and Peg — met the next week at Comfort's place. Sandy Niblet and Sarah Burk were there as well. As the company became increasingly drunk, the conversation once again turned to burning and killing. Only Sandy seemed afraid, so the band whetted knives and waved them in his face. Threatened with decapitation if he did not accede to the demands of the older slaves, he reluctantly agreed. The meetings had all taken place in the late afternoon and had ended by sundown, probably no later than five o'clock. Only later did Jack learn that Jack Sleydell had set fire to Murray's haystack and that Cato Provoost had set another fire, as had Cuffee Gomez. Cuffee did not have to worry about Jack's accusations. He, along with Cook and Robin Chambers and Caesar Peck, were executed before Jack had finished telling his tale to the court.

Quaco Roosevelt and Cuffee Philipse had confessed at the execution site, too late to save themselves. Jack's confession came after his conviction and saved him. Knowing that his compliance had prolonged his life, at least for the time being, other accused slaves rushed to tell the grand jury what they knew — or thought they knew, based on what others had told them — about the conspiracy. The early birds might live, whereas those who waited were sure to die. Pompey Leffert was the first to confess. He had heard about the plan to set fire to the town during a passing conversation with Quash Rutgers and Quaco Roosevelt. Quash had told Pompey that Ben Marshall also knew about the plan. For his presence of mind in stepping forward, Pompey would be spared the noose and sold and sent to Madeira. Recalled by the grand jury, Jack Comfort repeated the names of slaves present at Hughson's and Comfort's: one of the Spanish Negroes named Powlis, who was also known as Pablo, was not at Comfort's place, and Cato Cowley was not at Hughson's, but DeLancey's Antonio was at both.

The examinations and confessions had grown so numerous and fulsome that all Horsmanden had to do was refer to them by deponent and date. Thus, Pompey's confession was confirmed by Sandy's examination, "number three, section 8," and by Sarah Burk's "examination no. 2, June 1." Indeed, Horsmanden was so eager to show the confirmations from the cross-references that he added the following to his entry for June 9: "Worcester (Varian's) examination, June 22, 30," an event that had not yet happened and a witness not yet in custody! The court also controlled the time and use of these confessions. For example, the trial of the Hughsons was delayed for days so that Sandy Niblet's and Fortune Wilkins's confessions could be heard and then matched with other slaves' accounts. In all this, no slave was ever tried alone. They came and went in batches, small bands of men in chains. The court denied them the dignity of individual trials, though it sought their individual confessions.

In modern trials a defendant and the defendant's counsel have ways of manipulating time, gaining delays in order to better prepare their case. The extreme examples of the latter occur when defendant, counsel, or key witnesses for the defense are sick or otherwise unable to take part in the trial. None of this applied to the defendants in the New York cases. Time was entirely on the side of the court, and it chose to race through the trials by disposing of the defendants four or five at a time.

With their fellow slaves tripping over one another in their haste to confess and accuse, slave defendants at the bar who persisted in claiming their innocence could do precious little to save themselves. All they could offer, in Horsmanden's words, was a "defense as usual" based on denial. So Jack Comfort joined Sandy Niblet, Sarah Burk, and Mary Burton as witnesses for the prosecution, and the trial of Bastian Varick, Francis Bosch, Albany, and Curaçao Dick lasted but the morning of June 10 and ended in the same result as all the others.

Modern trials for serious crimes result in guilty verdicts less than 50 percent of the time. Often the defendants are able to plea-bargain the offense down and avoid the trial. Plea bargains were common in colonial criminal proceedings as well. Conviction rates for serious crimes in the colonies exceeded 60 percent, but only in cases involving slaves, pirates, and accused witches did the conviction rate ever approach 100 percent. In the conspiracy trials there were no acquittals, a situation only matched by the Salem witchcraft trials held during the spring and summer of 1692. If one were to include all the prosecutions for witchcraft begun in the spring of 1692 and ending in May of the following year, one would arrive at a mere 15 percent conviction rate for that offense. The conviction rate of the slaves in New York City was thus without precedent in colonial jury trials (or, for that matter, freeholders' courts for slaves in the colony).

Given the obstacles the court placed in the path of their defense and the legal talent arrayed against them — not to mention facing juries whose antipathy was manifest — the conviction rate may have been inevitable. But the fact that not one slave was acquitted still requires some comment. The conviction of the slaves who spoke up at Hughson's and Comfort's establishments was solely dependent on their presence and their words. One may rightly shudder at the idea that mere speech, particularly speech under the influence of alcohol, should be a capital offense. If a slave's threatening language reached the ears of the master, it would have been requited with corporal punishment, or perhaps the slave might have been sold to another owner. The slaves' words at Hughson's and Comfort's seemed particularly incendiary to the authorities because they were uttered by a group of slaves who had the relative freedom of movement to carry out the threat. It was not the words themselves but the context of their utterance that led the authorities to prosecute and the jury to vote to convict.

Foreseeing the outcome of his case, Bastian Varick could hardly contain himself in his eagerness to reveal what he had previously concealed. Confession and accusation had replaced stubborn silence as the slaves' common posture. According to Bastian, Hughson's wife and daughter were both present when Bastian swore to participate in the plot. They even used their family Bible to conduct the ceremony — on a Sunday, no less. All the executed slaves had been parties to the plot. Mary Burton had spoken truthfully. The motive behind the plot was expressed at the time by Caesar Varick as "to take the country." The plotters hoped that the Spanish and French would enter New York City and all the slaves would leave with the invaders. Bastian confirmed Jack Comfort's list of attendees at the two meetings. For his cooperation Bastian was pardoned. The terms of the pardon included Bastian's sale out of the colony to Hispaniola — a sentence of death by disease within two years for most slaves. At least he would not burn at the stake.

On June 12 the prosecution against Quash, Ben Marshall, Cato Peck, Cato Shurmur, and Fortune Vanderspiegle began. Mink Groesbeck, London Kelly, Mars Becker, Primus DeBrosse, Tom Rowe, Sterling Lawrence, Quamino Pemberton, and Bill Ten Eyck were arrested. The next day the two Antonios, Pablo, Juan (Wan), and Augustine, five of the Spanish Negroes, were arraigned, and Quash and his comrades were condemned to death. Pompey had joined Jack Comfort and Bastian Varick as a prosecution witness. They now had a lot of company.

Tickle Carpenter, knowing he would be part of the next batch of slaves brought to the court, followed Jack Comfort's and Bastian Varick's example by testifying against the conspirators. Tickle claimed he was at Hughson's tavern when constable Joseph North interrupted the festivities in search of stolen goods. The slaves were "feasting." Tickle's term corresponds to other slaves' accounts of the victuals that Hughson laid out. Slave fare in the city was no better or worse than that of servants, and like servants they supplemented their diets by what they could buy and steal. When Hughson treated them to mutton, fowl, bread, and ale, he attracted slaves to his cause who might not otherwise have been interested in entering his door. A "feast" was a way of opening negotiations on important matters.

Tickle had been present at a second feast, which was held on a Wednesday at Hughson's tavern around the third week in January. Cato Cowley, London Kelly, the brewer's Mars, Indian Wan Low, Mink Groesbeck, Primus DeBrosse, and the usual crew were present, numbering some twenty or thirty in all. Hughson had taken the lead in organizing the conspiracy, for he wanted the stolen goods brought to his tavern when the fires had caused the houses to be emptied. Tickle's testimony throws some light on what Hughson's actual purpose may have been. He had no use for a slave uprising (even if he was to be proclaimed king in the new slave-run colony), and he probably did not enjoy the prospect of a race war. What he wanted was an increased flow of goods that he could fence. So he promised them drink and fed them, let them dance and gamble in his tavern, and proved his loyalty by exposing his family to the slaves' violent fantasies of rape and murder (though when they danced to Ben's fiddle, his wife and daughter remained apart from the slaves).

If only he could keep his tongue-wagging, boasting accessories quiet about the scheme. That was why he swore them to silence. They did keep silent, never revealing the plot to their masters, but among themselves there was no such thing as silence. In the streets, the fields, at work, at home, visiting, or "frolicking," they regaled one another with the plot as though it were a fable that improved with each telling. As one witness told the court, on Friday, July 10, "it was a common talk over the town and country, that Hughson was concerned in a plot with the Negroes."

Hughson not only underestimated the number of slaves who would soon learn of the plan but misunderstood the slaves' thinking. His primary contacts with the gangs — Caesar Varick and Prince Auboyneau — were thieves. Quaco Roosevelt was merely a malcontent. Hughson assumed he could command them. Jack Sleydell, another guest at Hughson's "supper," and Tickle Carpenter both stated that the slaves had had too much to drink, and that they "said to one another let us set fire to the town and kill the white people, and then we will make our escape." Hughson was listening, but to him it must have seemed no more than the grousing of angry, tired men. Hughson, however, did not reckon on Ben Marshall and some of the others. They were genuine revolutionaries who thought, at least while in their cups, that they might overturn an oppressive regime and thereby gain their freedom.

The parade of slaves herded into the jails, called before the grand jury, sent up to the courtroom, and shortly thereafter transported to the execution ground continued throughout the month of June. A few, like Mink Groesbeck and Tom Moore, pleaded guilty at their arraignment, but most still maintained their innocence at this early stage of the proceedings. When Pedro DePeyster, Fortune Vanderspiegle, Tony Latham, and Prince Crooke were committed, however, Prince immediately confessed. He and York Marschalk had attended the execution of Cuffee Philipse, and York said that now was the time to rise up in rebellion. Surrounded as they were by whites whose delight in the burning at the stake of Cuffee was all too apparent, Prince demurred. It was hardly the right time to do anything of the sort. York was infuriated by the scene; Prince was sobered by it. The court did not make such distinctions: every slave who attended the meetings and was sworn to join the insurrection was treated the same.

The Spanish Negroes retained some sense of their distinction from the others — and of their rights as well. They told the court that they were free men in their own land, wrongfully enslaved and thus illegally sold to masters in New York. They insisted that the indictments identify them by their proper names: Antonio de St. Benedito, Antonio de la Cruz, Pablo Venture Angel, Juan de la Silvia, and Augustine Gutierrez. Still, they could not speak or understand English and thus could not conduct their defense without assistance. Moreover, how could Mary Burton testify against them when she could not understand a word they said? Perhaps, like Ben Marshall, they were insurrectionists, but they insisted on a fair trial.

The trial began on June 17, with Mordecai Gomez, a Sephardic Jew, serving as interpreter. Burton could not testify to what the Spanish Negroes had said, but she swore that Hughson had told her they would burn down Captain Lush's house. Other slaves within her hearing had said that the Spanish Negroes were part of the plot and could fight well. Sandy Niblet testified that at least one of the defendants could speak enough English to point to Lush's house and make threats. Juan and Pablo could also make themselves understood in English, and they, too, had damned Lush. Jack Comfort confirmed Sandy's testimony, as did Tickle Carpenter and Bastian Varick. Captain Lush himself was sworn in by the court — under the law, slaves could not testify under oath — and testified that the Spanish men could speak some English.

Of all the defendants, only Antonio de St. Benedito, Peter DeLancey's man, had what seemed to be an airtight alibi, and DeLancey provided it. Antonio had spent the entire winter at DeLancey's farm outside of the city, had gotten frostbite on his toes, and could barely walk. He did not return to the city until after the fire at the fort. The others had a different alibi. They were ill and bedridden for most of the winter. Jacob Sarly testified that his slave Juan rarely went out at night because of illness. Frederick Becker, master of Pablo, said his man was ill throughout the month of March. Augustine's master not only gave him a good character reference but averred that Augustine, too, was ill and did not travel about until Easter. Proof of the defendants' "nightwalking" (an offense under the slave code) was of vital importance, for the prosecution believed that slaves could travel about at night virtually unseen because of their dark skin color. In fact, some of the slaves did move about at night to visit other slaves, drink at taverns, and steal. For example, Will Ward, another of the suspects, had asked Jack Tiebout if he could construct a lantern cover consisting of wooden planks that "nobody could see."

The jury, however, was not swayed — neither by the prisoners' protestations nor by the testimony of their masters. As Burton and the other witnesses avowed, even if the Spanish Negroes were virtually housebound, they could still have given their assent to the plot if they had attended the feast at Hughson's tavern (which the slaves were now calling "the great supper") and the drinking spree at

Comfort's. It took barely a half hour (Horsmanden recorded the time) for the jury to retire, deliberate on all five cases, and return with a guilty verdict.

The trials of the five Spanish Negroes were unremarkable in one respect (no one was found innocent in these trials) but quite remarkable in another: they had turned the world of colonial status and authority upside down. The rank of the character witnesses outside the courtroom and the evidence of men like Peter DeLancey should, under ordinary circumstances, have swayed a jury. Many jurors had business dealings with the DeLanceys, owed them money or depended on them for credit, and voted for them for office. The DeLanceys expected deference from such men. Although many men and women refused to bow to the powerful, most others did. Colonial judges and juries in particular routinely noted the status of litigants in lawsuits. Assuming that the deference usually given men of their standing would protect their slaves from conviction, DeLancey and his ilk provided them with alibis.

Horsmanden noted that many of the slaves in the cells or the dock had shown through their facial expressions and comments that they expected their masters to intercede for them. Masters routinely did this, even in times of impending or rumored insurrection. Either they did not believe their loyal bondsmen could be part of such a plot, took what their slaves said to them at face value, or simply did not want to lose the value of a slave trained to a craft or regarded as part of a household. Allowing masters to testify was a "great indulgence" to them, for they had an interest in the outcome of the case that could easily skew their testimony. (In civil cases, under the common law, parties with a financial interest in the outcome were not allowed to testify in court.) But Horsmanden jeered at such masters for their credulity and feared that allowing masters to take a formal part in the proceedings would lead to "proceedings much retarded by the spectators asking many questions of the prisoners and witnesses, and some of them not proper." What judges found in the latter case was that masters "were prone to countenance and excuse their slaves." But the masters' intercession in the case of the five Spanish Negroes did not help the slaves — proving once again that slave law was a category unto itself.

The case of Othello, Chief Justice James DeLancey's valet, partially illustrates why customary forms of deference did not function at these trials. Othello was convicted and executed even though he had nothing to do with setting the fires or participating in the burglaries. Accompanying his master outside the colony when the fires were set, he had merely kept silent about the plot. Horsmanden conceded that Othello was a man of decency and dignity, but he was not truly forthcoming even when he finally confessed, and his refusal to name names could not be tolerated.

Indeed, it was because Othello had such an "indulgent master" (here Horsmanden was paying court to James DeLancey, Horsmanden's patron in colonial politics) that the slave's complicity was all the more censurable. DeLancey had taken "a great deal of pains with him, endeavoring to persuade him to confess if he was any way engaged in" the plot, but "Othello withstood it all" — even the promise DeLancey made to intercede with the lieutenant governor to gain Othello mercy. In remaining silent for so long, Othello was choosing loyalty to the other slaves over loyalty to his master.

Innocence and guilt had nothing to do with the matter. Othello would be convicted if he pleaded not guilty and spared if he acknowledged his guilt. Some historians have suggested that his silence was based on racial solidarity or class attachment. In all probability, it was loyalty to friends. One should bear in mind that Othello's status, as butler to DeLancey, was as high as any slave in the colony. The court believed that all the other slaves looked up to him, as they did not to scoundrels like Caesar Varick and wastrels like Jack Comfort. Thus, by holding out on the court even after he had confessed, Othello became a model for other slaves. Ironically, the court felt it had to make him "a lesson" to the other slaves. DeLancey understood this, as did Othello. It is not easy to decide who demonstrated the greater degree of dignity on this occasion, the slave or the master.

By now few slaves pleaded not guilty when their turn came. Gathered together in the jail cells beneath the city hall, able to talk to one another, and well aware of the fates of those who had gone to trial already, the slaves either changed their pleas to guilty and begged for clemency from the court or confessed and turned informer before their trial began. As Horsmanden sneered, "Now many Negroes began to squeak."

More astute slaves assayed another line of defense. Combining penitence and confession, they averred that they were besotted with drink when they assented to the conspiracy. Scipio Bound, a defendant "that did not want sense, and had had a better education than most of his colour" according to Horsmanden, made the most of this defense during his examination on July 2. At Hughson's tavern he had agreed to the plan, "but it was with me as it is with all my colour, who are never easy till they get a dram, and when they have one want more; this was my case on my meeting with Comfort's Jack, who carried me to Hughson's." There, already drunk, Scipio drank more and, "bewitched with drink," said things that he would never have said while sober. Scipio also took the precaution of bringing his Bible with him, which he clutched to his chest. Scipio's defense not only saved his life but persuaded the court to do something about the whites who had supplied slaves with liquor in violation of the laws. On July 23 a parade of whites, including a number of women, were presented to the court, summarily tried and convicted, and fined for "keeping a disorderly house, entertaining Negroes, etc."

The bulk of the slave confessions occurred in the middle or latter portion of June and in early July. They had resulted in the arrest of thirty more slaves by the end of June. The newly arrested slaves immediately pleaded guilty and "submitted to the mercy of the court." The confessions shared common elements: meetings by accident rather than by design; rumor rather than deliberation; casual rather than premeditated membership in the loose affiliation of disaffected slaves. Often one or more of the confederates would be in his cups. They took a walk, stopped to drink, demanded of one another if they knew, and if they knew were they man enough to go through with the plot. A few, like Jack Comfort and Ben Marshall, seemed to take the lead. Like those at the apex of a charitable organization, they delegated recruiting and similar menial chores to others.

The court rewarded the confessors by offering them a reprieve and commuting their sentence, almost always accompanied by their sale and transportation out of the colony. Only five of the eighty-one slaves who confessed were executed, and all of these confessions took place just before the slaves were to be executed.

They also came from men like Will Ward, whose history of

involvement in plots elsewhere finally caught up with him. Will's case was unique in the docket. As Linebaugh and Rediker discovered, Will was involved in an insurrection on Saint John's, located in the West Indies. Over 146 slaves were named as conspirators, and 27 were executed for their part in that 1733 rebellion, yet Will was simply sold off. Two years later he was caught plotting a rebellion on Antigua. He now saved his neck by informing on his comrades. He was sold again, this time to New York, and arrived in time to join the 1741 conspiracy. He was either an inveterate troublemaker or a committed revolutionary, but the court was not interested in his motives.

Of those who pleaded not guilty at the end of June and the beginning of July, Tony Latham, Chief Justice DeLancey's slave Othello, and Galloway Rutgers were hanged. (In fact, friends of the court had to petition it to change the sentence of death from burning to hanging, and this after the court refused to petition the lieutenant governor to pardon the slaves because their confessions had come too late and seemed insincere). Slaves who hedged their confessions also did not fare well, like Quack Walter who was hanged. Submission — abject, total, and forthright — was required and had to precede conviction.

If, by the end of June, submission was proving to be an effectual bar to execution, what explains the change of heart by the court from harshness to leniency? It might have been the fact that the execution of so many slaves — by the last week of June the total had risen to nineteen — had moved the court to mercy. The ringleaders were all gone now, or so it seemed; there was one more ringleader Horsmanden would discover, but his identity had not yet been revealed. Only eleven more supposed conspirators were executed in the remaining trials, almost all of the men persisting in their denials of guilt.

A few slaves even convinced the grand jury that they were simply passive listeners while others plotted. Kid Van Horn, Hereford Cohen, and Tom Van Zant were discharged by the grand jury on July 2, and on July 23 the grand jury dismissed John Francois, a free black, along with slaves Tom Valet, Dick Robins, Dublin Walton, Quack Goelet, Will Tiebout, Junio Van Courtlandt, Diego Marschalk, and Diego Vandursen. Earlier the grand jury had been fervent in its commitment to ferret out every conspirator. Now it proved more cautious than the trial juries. The reason may simply be that the grand juries heard cases individually. Thus, slaves coming before them retained their individuality. As the fever of suspicion cooled, the grand jurors were better able to distinguish between active and passive participants. The trial juries never once heard the case of an individual slave. Every trial included multiple defendants, who remained indistinct, a category rather than a collection of individuals.

On July 4, 1741, with the jail overflowing with slaves who had confessed and the authorities fearing the outbreak of some terrible pestilence, the court drew up a list of those slaves who might be pardoned en masse at the lieutenant governor's discretion. Forty-two were named for reprieve and transportation, among them Sarah Burk, Patrick English, Fortune Wilkins, and Scipio Bound. On July 9 the court heard them plead their pardons and ordered their masters, on pain of forfeiture of a fifty-pound bond, to transport the slaves abroad.

What was to be done about Sarah Hughson Jr.? She had not been as forthcoming in confessing as Jack, Tickle, or Prince. Horsmanden hinted at the possibility that she might have been mildly retarded. Lunatics and idiots were rarely held responsible for their actions in English courts. Or she may still have been in shock over the fate of her parents. In any case, offered the chance to save herself by accusing her parents, and by "configuring what had hitherto been unfolded concerning this accursed scheme . . . she was a wretch stupefied and hardened in wickedness, and seemed void of all sense of a future state." The judges wished she would say something — they knew that in law as well as in fact she had little volition in the entire affair and should not be judged as culpable as her parents — but all they could do was to move her execution a week after her father's and mother's execution in the hope that their example would loosen her tongue. More important, she must bow to their authority by asking for mercy. Her reprieve was continued until July 29, when she was pardoned. Her testimony, the court had decided, would prove vital in the conviction of a conspirator whose presence in the affair was only briefly and inconsequentially noticed before late June.

On April 14, in the midst of a welter of indictments of slaves for conspiracy, the grand jury indicted "one John Ury" a "suspected priest" for "having come into the province of New York" and against its statutes "celebrated masses and granted absolutions." There was no mention of a connection between him and the conspiracy—not yet—but there soon would be.

CHAPTER 7

The Trial of the Suspected Priest

There was one final trial, unanticipated at the start of the drama and outwardly not following the trajectory of the rest of the conspiracy. It was more a denouement than a climax. In retrospect, the defendant should have been regarded as a minor character introduced late in the story. He had little stature as a performer and no status in the white or black communities. Yet the trial of John Ury, suspected of being a Roman Catholic priest and inciting the slaves to rebel, was to Horsmanden and the rest of the elite bar a signal event. It bestowed an international dimension on what had thus far been a sad and sordid local affair by indicting the despised Catholic enemy for the slave uprising. In the minds of his prosecutors, Ury's participation in the events tied the slave conspiracy to the conspiratorial designs of the hated and feared papacy and its most trusted agent, the Spanish.

The most worrisome charge against the Spanish Negroes had been that they might link hands with the Roman Catholic Spanish enemy. England was at war with Spain in the summer of 1741, raising the old fear of the Roman Catholic "fifth column" within the colony. That fear had a long history in English minds, for England had been at war with Spain, off and on, since Elizabeth I confirmed the Protestant succession in 1558. In the ensuing years, Elizabeth set her "sea dogs" — men like Francis Drake and John Hawkins — to prey on the Spanish possessions in the Caribbean and in Central and South America. The Spanish sent a fleet against England in 1588, but it was defeated at sea and wrecked by a storm on the way home. Warfare between the two nations continued sporadically for the next century and a half as England and Spain sparred for control of the Caribbean.

Although the major reason for the English-Spanish conflict in the New World was the contest for riches, religious differences contributed to the ferocity. Contests between Roman Catholics and Protestants begun in the Reformation had plunged Europe into nearly two centuries of civil wars. England was a leader among the Protestant powers and Spain was the most determined defender of Roman Catholicism in Europe. That conflict spilled over into the New World colonies as soon as England established a foothold in Virginia. Although the Spanish never invaded the English mainland colonies, they planned such incursions on more than one occasion.

The English assumed that the papacy and the Spanish relied on information supplied by Roman Catholics in England and its colonies. Roman Catholics lived in the British Isles (they were a majority in southern Ireland) and throughout the British Empire, but they could not hold office and their Protestant neighbors never trusted them. During the English Restoration (1660–88) the crown had attempted to promote tolerance for English Catholics in the empire. Indeed, James, duke of York, who ruled England as James II (1685–88) was a Roman Catholic. His plans for toleration went far beyond what his Protestant countrymen would allow, however, and became one of the reasons he was deposed in 1688.

Parliament did pass an act of toleration when James left England, but its beneficiaries were dissenting Protestant sects like the Congregationalists and the Presbyterians. The Church of England remained the state church to which everyone who wished to hold office had to swear allegiance. After 1688 Catholics worshiped in private, and Roman Catholic priests were forbidden to officiate at masses. Periodically English Protestants indulged in anti–Roman Catholic pogroms, suspecting all English Roman Catholics of being more loyal to England's Catholic enemies like Spain than to England itself. In the 1690s Catholics were forbidden to own guns except those they needed to protect their homes. In 1714 Parliament again ordered local magistrates to disarm the Catholics.

Roman Catholics were persecuted throughout the English colonies, even in Maryland, a colony they had created. In New England they were believed to be devil worshipers. In Georgia they were accused of plotting with the Spanish in neighboring Florida, a Spanish colony, to overthrow the government. New Yorkers had a special reason to fear the Roman Catholics in their midst: Catholic French

Canada perched on New York's northern border like a bird of prey. King William's War (1688–97) and Queen Anne's War (1701–13) brought bloodshed to the colony as French and Indian raiders, often accompanied by Roman Catholic priests or Jesuit missionaries, overran Schenectady and menaced Albany in the Hudson and Mohawk valleys. The current war with Spain would surely lead to war with France (which came to pass in 1744) and that war would rage along the New York frontier. New York authorities especially hated the Jesuits — this despite the fact that the Jesuits often intervened to save the lives of captives — for the same Jesuits joined with churchmen in Canada to attempt to convert New York captives to Catholicism. As Horsmanden wrote to Cadwallader Colden on August 7, 1741, "There is scarce a plot but a priest is at the bottom of it."

In 1741 the English raised troops in New York to join a British naval expedition against the Spanish on the coast of South America. In the spring the newspapers were filled with accounts of the campaign. Fever had broken out among the New York volunteers, and many in the city feared that their loved ones would never return from the expedition. The distrust of Catholics at home was heightened by the publication in May of a letter from Governor James Oglethorpe of Georgia to Lieutenant Governor Clarke. William Smith Jr.'s history of New York reported that the letter arrived on May 16, 1741, just as Oglethorpe was preparing to invade Spanish Florida. Oglethorpe feared that agents of Spain — including slaves converted to Catholicism and priests concealing their identities — had infiltrated the English colonies. He shared with Clarke rumors that the Spanish were employing runaway slaves to destroy English powder magazines.

Clarke was less afraid of slave runaways than the "many priests" whom Oglethorpe reported "were employed, [or] who pretended to be physicians, dancing masters, and other such kinds of occupations" in order to gain positions of trust in the English colonies. They could then act as mentors to the slaves in sabotaging the English colonial fortifications when the Spanish fleet arrived. Horsmanden was concerned that "intimation having been given for some time past, that there had been of late Popish priests lurking about the town." In fact, a colony law dating from the time of King William's War made it a crime for Catholic priests to practice in the colony (for fear they would turn the Indians against the English crown). The wartime measure was still on the books, nearly half a century later, when Ury was arrested. As he told Colden, Horsmanden was ready to believe that some priest was "a principal promoter and encourager of this most horrible and detestable piece of villainy."

Mary Burton provided the first clue to the connection between Ury and the slave conspiracy. Perhaps her testimony should have been regarded with skepticism. She was always there with the convenient hint or clue. At the same time, she had no need to lie; she had done her part. Perhaps, like the young accusers of witches at Salem, she had grown so used to the spotlight that she was addicted to it. In any case, she identified the priest as "one Ury, alias Jury." Over the course of three years — from 1741 until he finished his account in 1744 — Horsmanden assembled some of the facts of Ury's life. An immigrant from England, he had formed a partnership in New York City with a schoolmaster named John Campbell to teach Latin and Greek. Knowledge of both languages was required for students wishing to enter college in the colonies or in England. (In effect, the classical languages were the SATs of the day.)

Ury was arrested and presented to Burton, who confirmed that he had often visited Hughson's tavern, sometimes staying the night in one of the upstairs rooms. Since he left early in the morning, Burton hardly spoke to him, usually rising after he was gone. He was present when the plot was discussed, however, and seemed on intimate terms with Hughson and his family, as well as with Peg. Sometimes he whispered in Hughson's ear. Although he never spoke out on these occasions, Burton ventured the opinion that "his actions and behavior" signified his approbation. According to Burton, Ury took pains not to be overheard by her (often carrying on his conversations in one of the upper rooms), and she (despite attempts to eavesdrop) had never heard him say that he was a priest. In what was clearly embellishment — she had already indicated that Ury suspected her and did not speak about the plot in her presence — she added that Ury had offered her silks "and a deal of fine things" if she would swear to join the conspirators.

Burton also placed Campbell, Garritt Van Emborough, and Antonio de St. Benedito in Ury's company. In the course of her denunciation of Ury, Burton admitted to her relationship with the slaves who frequented the tavern. On more than one occasion they had "behaved rudely towards her [or] provoked her." A court with a little more objective distance from the proceedings (that is, one that did not act as judge and prosecution combined) might have weighed her testimony against the slaves differently in light of this admission. They frightened her, threatened her, and made unwanted advances toward her, so accusing them was one way of paying them back. In its haste to ferret out demonic Catholicism, the court did not hear her inadvertent but telling indication of her rancor against the slaves, instead taking note of Ury's remark to her that he could forgive her sins as well as theirs.

Embellishment had become common in the slaves' testimony, as though the deponents were trying to outdo one another in terms of outrageous confessions in the same way that, before the fire at the fort, they had tried to outdo one another in their boasts concerning the violent overthrow of their masters. Burton might have embroidered her tales, but she could not match the creativity of slave Adam Murray. Horsmanden remarked that the inquisitors had a hard time getting Adam to talk, but once he did he grew fond of his own voice.

The magistrates listened to Adam spin his tales for hours on end over the course of several days. After all, he had shown his guilt by his distracted behavior long before he was arrested. Soon Adam, who knew all about the lieutenant governor's proclamation, had made himself as indispensable to the prosecution as Jack Comfort, Sandy Niblet, and Sarah Burk. Adam became a marvelously fulsome penitent whose tales of meetings and frolics among the conspirators mixed the ribald and the horrifying.

More important, Adam was the next witness to mention Ury. The schoolmaster, "a little short man," was often at Hughson's tavern. Hughson told Adam that Ury "was one of the two priests who could forgive sins." Adam suspected that Ury was a party to the plot, but did not hear him say so. Why Hughson would have confided Ury's great secret to Adam, whose gift of gab could hardly be constrained by any oath, was unclear.

Adam knew Ury as a schoolteacher, one of a number of whites

involved in the plot. (The other was the dancing master, one Holt, at least according to Holt's slave Joe.) But there was stronger evidence against Ury than Adam's or Joe Holt's testimony. It came from the mouth of William Kane, an Irish soldier who frequented Hughson's tavern. He was forty and had lived in the colony for four and a half years, was married, and (after an initial denial), admitted to knowing Ury. Although he could not write his own name, he could name names, and Ury's was one of them.

It all began after duty one night at the fort, when Kane, drunk, accompanied stableman Jerry Corker, another Irishman, to the cockfights. Kane learned from his companion that there would be a "Romish" priest there, and that after the fights a christening would take place. Three days later (the cockfights were a regular diversion for the troops), Kane met the priest, a "little man" who lodged at Corker's place. At Hughson's tavern Kane joined the plot to burn the city. Along with Hughson's mother-in-law (a cunning woman said to be a folk healer and prophetess but considered "crazy"), Hughson's father, and his three brothers. No one else had accused the rest of the Hughson men, and this was probably more embroidery. But Kane was doing what the slaves had shied away from — bringing whites into the plot — and it made his testimony more frightening to the court.

Corker was Catholic, and Kane, who loudly protested his Protestantism, accused Corker of trying to convert him. Supposedly that was what all Catholics tried to do to Protestants. Catholic priests and lay people in Canada did try to convert Protestant captives and prisoners of war, so Kane's story had a touch of verisimilitude even if it was not not wholly believable in its detail. For if a secret band of Catholics constituted the real movers and shakers behind a plot to burn down the city, why did none of the slave defendants name Corker as a regular at Hughson's? (Much the same can be said for the absence of Ury up to this time.) It may have been that Kane, "reputed a papist," was trying to divert suspicion from himself. Indeed, he saw Catholics everywhere: John Coffin (a peddler who kept a house in the city), Edward Kelly, Peter Connolly, Edward Murphy, and David Johnson. All, according to Kane, were secret Catholics and plotters.

Kane swore that Ury had been at the center of the schemes and was among the most ambitious. For example, he wanted to delay a plan to burn down the "English Church last Christmas" until the roof had dried and more worshipers were present. Kane next named all the slaves who were involved in the plot, including Jack Comfort, Quack Walter, Harry (a "Negro doctor"), Sandy Niblet, and the gang that met at Hughson's tavern.

Horsmanden and the court now had bigger fish to fry than Niblet, and daughter Sarah Hughson, facing the final hours of her life, grudgingly helped them do it. On July 8, while both women awaited the court's pleasure concerning their impending execution, Sarah Hughson confessed to Sarah Burk that Hughson knew all about the plan to burn down the city. Burk relayed the news to the undersheriff, who told the judges, who summoned young Hughson. This time she confessed, putting both Kane and Ury at the center of her story. Kane had been sworn in by her father and Ury was often seen drinking with the Negroes. More she would not say, and the court reluctantly sent her back to the jail cells.

Between the testimonies of Burton and Kane the court was amassing considerable evidence against Ury and his alleged ring of Catholic incendiaries. Burton named soldiers Edward Murphy and Andrew Ryan. Kane added Andrew Johnson, a hatter, and said that Saint Patrick's Day was chosen for the incineration of the city. Coffin and John Earl, another soldier, often brought stolen goods to Hughson's tavern. According to Othello DeLancey, many soldiers, including Tom Evans and James O'Brien, came there during their off hours with stolen goods in their hands and larceny in their hearts. All the while, according to Kane (who traveled in circles closed to Burton), Ury was acting as a priest, christening children and chanting prayers.

Sarah Hughson finally found her voice, adding that John Ury had christened Caesar Varick "and others." Peg was now revealed as a Catholic, and Sarah Jr. was sworn into the plot, though she had not converted. Ury had told all of them that as a priest he could forgive their sins, including those of arson and murder. She suspected that he had converted her parents and knew that he had prayed with the slaves at her father's house. Indeed, he heard confessions there, turning it into a chapel. Horsmanden and the other judges found her revelations trustworthy, though she was wont to retract the next day what she had said the day before. How extensive was the Catholic plot? Thomas Hughson, the tavern keeper's father, and four of John Hughson's brothers — Nathaniel, Walter, William, and Richard — were all arrested lest they spread the contagion farther.

This was the worst fear of the authorities, for if the two plots overlapped, with the slaves becoming pawns in a scheme that Roman Catholics had arranged, the danger to the city increased significantly. The whites never believed that slaves could effectively organize the overthrow of the government or the destruction of the town. William Smith Sr. and others felt that such assumptions on the part of slaves were a combination of buffoonery and effrontery. Hughson's leadership had made the plot more plausible, and he was a monster for his supposed part in it, but he, no more than they, expected to succeed. How could a petty crook and a column of slaves bring down a crown colony? Roman Catholics ruled much of Europe, however, and had waged war against Protestant England and her colonies for a century. The Spanish enemy was Catholic and had used Catholic slaves to serve as its agents.

Moreover, rumors of a Roman Catholic–led plot in the city had to be respected, for Roman Catholics — priests in particular — were assumed to be veteran, wily, and totally committed plotters, practiced at conspiracy, lying, and secrecy. Indeed, in this sense Ury's late appearance in the plot weighed against him. Ordinarily he might have argued in his defense that if he had been so prominent, why had all the informers not named him in May or June? But if adeptness at secrecy was a characteristic of Catholic plotters, his protracted invisibility was but one more proof of his complicity.

Some of the slave confessions now began to mention a Catholic priest among the white people at Hughson's tavern. Apparently word of Ury's predicament had reached the jail cells under the city hall, and slaves awaiting their fate seized the opportunity to denounce the supposed Roman Catholic plot. Bastian, for example, had seen Kane with a Roman Catholic priest and had heard that the priest had sworn slaves into the plot and promised to forgive them their sins. Ury was replacing Hughson as the key figure in the conspiracy. Conspirators included a shadowy cadre of whites: the soldiers Kane, Kelly, Murphy, Ryan, and Connolly; the dancing masters Holt and Corry; and various marginal figures in the city economy, such as hatters, journeymen, and peddlers like Johnson and Coffin. Above all, behind them stood Ury, the master marionettist. The slaves, by comparison, were receding into the background as more and more of them pleaded for mercy and were freed upon their masters' promise to transport them out of the colony.

———

With the more grandiose dimensions of imagined slave rebellions temporarily pushed to the side, the proceedings took on the familiar face of capital trials of the king's subjects. The defendants could all speak English and knew their rights as subjects of the crown. The bombastic, righteous language the court had used to condemn the slaves vanished, replaced with the hard-edged, realistic jargon of courts in England. The judges began to confront one white witness's testimony with another's: Corry's with Kane's, Kane's with Burton's. Finally it was Ury's turn. He asked for pen and paper to compose his defense, plus a copy of the indictments against him. One cannot know for sure whether his knowledge of classical languages aided him, but he had no intention of conceding anything to the court. Ury denied everything, including any acquaintance with Hughson, but Kane had told the grand jury that Ury, Coffin, Corker, Daniel Fagen, and Thomas Hughson were part of the plot. Fagen and Corry had fled, prudently, given how easily the innocent could find themselves in the dock when so much depended on such unreliable friends.

The grand jury found Ury guilty of inciting slaves to set fire to the fort and of violating an act of the assembly passed in 1699 "for that he being an ecclesiastical person, made by authority pretended from the see of Rome, did . . . come into the province and city of New-York, and there remained for the space of seven months." Under the terms of the act, it did not matter whether Ury was an ordained priest so long as he pretended to be one "by practicing and teaching of others to say any Popish prayers, by celebrating masses, granting of absolutions, or using any other of the Romish ceremonies, and rites of worship." The penalty for the latter offense was "perpetual imprisonment." This is the only offense for which such a sentence existed under colonial law, making it, like slavery, a category unto itself. Attempting to break out of jail after one's conviction on the offense was a capital crime punishable by death.

Ury's journal had been seized when he was arrested, and his itinerary was copied from it. He had arrived in the colonies in 1738 through the port city of Philadelphia and had proceeded north. There was nothing in the journal about a plot, but there were entries that proved he had acted in a clerical capacity the previous year. In May 1741 he officiated at the "baptism" of Timothy Ryan, who was one year old at the time. Why Ryan had not been baptized earlier was a matter that Horsmanden considered important — indeed, it proved that Ryan's parents were Catholics and were waiting for a priest to perform the ceremony. The father may have been the selfsame soldier Andrew Ryan named by Kane. A second sinister-sounding entry read, "Pater confessor Butler 2 Anni. Non sacramentum, non confessio." Whatever the entry may have meant, Horsmanden could not make sense of it other than to assume that Butler was Ury's confessor. Its very foreignness seemed to make it even more telling as evidence against Ury.

It is surely ill-advised at this remove to try to figure out what Ury meant, much less why he wrote it down. Assuming that the entry and the journal are not Horsmanden's fabrications (unlikely, because Horsmanden was writing only three years after the events and would have expected many in his audience to have known whether there was a journal and what it said) or an anonymous forgery, one can begin to piece together an explanation. It may be that Ury meant to say to Father Confessor Butler that it had been two years since Ury had received the sacrament of Eucharist (that is, Holy Communion, the partaking of wine and wafer at a Catholic mass) or undergone confession. Easter, when he wrote the entry, was a special time for observant Catholics to attend mass. If he were a priest, however, he could have celebrated the mass himself. Private ritual observance was one of the complaints that Protestants lodged against Catholic clergymen. Similarly, if he had pretended to be a priest and had celebrated mass, Ury would have had no need to write the entry. In fact, the passage seems exculpatory, a kind of confession in itself. But that seems to imply that Ury saw himself as a Catholic layman.

The entry may have been an admission that he could not offer mass properly for fear his disguise would be discovered. Catholic priests then were required to celebrate mass every day. Ury's entry probably meant that he was aware of this obligation and regretted its omission. But if he had been a priest, the omission would have been a grave dereliction of duty. If so, the entry could have been a draft of a confession that Ury intended to make to Father Butler, the sort of scribbling we often do to aid our memory. If this was its purpose, the entry would prove that Ury was a Catholic who looked forward to the time when he could properly confess his sins. But the most obvious explanation is that Ury had gone two years without receiving confession or communion. This would support the notion that he was a Catholic at heart but would not prove that he had presented himself to anyone as a priest. All in all, the entry does not support the prosecution's thesis that Ury was a priest, but it might support the supposition that he was practicing some of the rites of the church. In the end one is left with the picture of a man who yearned to be something he was not and who practiced a variety of religious rites that did not reflect the practices of any conventional sect.

John Chambers was selected as special prosecutor for the crown to aid Attorney General Bradley, but the case was postponed from day to day during the week of July 20. The purpose of the delay was to squeeze more information out of Sarah Hughson Jr. She suddenly recalled that before Christmas 1740 Ury had drawn a chalk circle on the floor, placing the slaves around it and standing in the middle with a cross in his hand, and had made the slaves swear not to reveal his identity. This supposedly explained why none of the confessed conspirators had named him in June. She had also seen Ury baptize the slaves and had heard him promise to forgive them their sins for the plot. She also overheard slaves say that they had visited Ury's lodgings to pray with him. Finally, she recalled that Ury had tried to convert her. Although she had been obdurate in the matter of her parents, if she "kept to her history" in testimony against Ury the court promised to recommend her for pardon. On July 27 she was spared.

Testimony by Elias DeBrosse, a confectioner, seemed to indicate that Ury was looking for sacramental wafers for the mass. Because of the French name, Ury may have thought that DeBrosse was a secret Catholic. In any case, he dropped into the shop to ask if DeBrosse could bake wafers like those used by Lutheran priests in their ceremonies. DeBrosse, curious, asked if Ury was a minister and where his congregation might be, but Ury merely waved him off and left the store. Joseph Webb, a carpenter, testified that at the cockfights that Corker hosted, Webb had heard Ury reading Latin, whereupon Webb sent his son to study with Ury. Ury and the carpenter soon became friends, with Ury often dining at Webb's house. (Webb noted that Ury had few possessions and looked poor.) But in the course of a conversation on religion Ury "expressed himself in a such a dark, obscure, and mysterious manner, that the deponent could not understand him." Webb had introduced Ury to DeBrosse and had witnessed the odd conversation between them about the wafers.

Ury had also told Webb that blacks had souls that could be saved, though they had a "slavish nature" and were meant to serve white men. Ury preached within Webb's hearing, but he did so according to the rites of the Church of England, and then only on topics of personal morality. Ury also thought that people should be allowed to worship as they chose and to attend those services they preferred.

On another occasion, Ury had supposedly warned that faith without good works denied the efficacy of God's justice and mercy, a belief that confuted basic Calvinist doctine. Calvinists, including the reform English Protestants, believed that God had "elected" those who were saved and that the true Christian church was a gathering of the saved. Congregationalists and Presbyterians accepted this doctrine, although itinerant preachers during the Great Awakening had raised the possibility that the number of saved might be enormous and that penitent sinners should look for proof of their salvation within their own hearts. Ury's sermon was aimed at the Presbyterians in the city, a strong party which included William Smith and other Morrisites.

But Ury seemed to be arguing that the church itself, through its sacraments, could save, which was a Roman Catholic rather than a Protestant position. Such a stance assigned to priests of the church — and the mass service — the role of intermediary in the salvation process, a role that Calvinism declined to give its ministers. They might help prepare the congregant, but they and the church were not the Body of Christ on earth and could not save. Only God could save, and perfect faith was the only true proof of salvation. No sacraments, like taking mass or confession, however holy or charitable, aided in salvation, though the saved proved themselves, in part, through their righteousness on earth. Webb thought that Ury had said he administered the sacraments but was not certain.

Today the prosecution must prove its case beyond a reasonable doubt. The case against Ury was filled with uncertainty. Who was this little man who had been accused of so much evil? During his last days in jail, he told a gentleman caller that he was the son of a director of the South Sea Company, one of England's greatest investment enterprises, but that his father had died before becoming wealthy. Ury said he had been reared by a dissenting clergyman (that is, a minister not affiliated with the Church of England), had attended two universities, had preached at a chapel in England, but, having written a book condemning the Church of England, had lost his pulpit and his prospects, and had thus come to America — quite a story. Inquiries made in England after Ury's death turned up a gentleman who knew him and his family. The father was indeed a businessman whose death had left the family destitute. Ury was indeed very religious, but he had no formal training in any field, held no pulpit, and had written no book. He had come to America to make his fortune.

What should one make of all this? Ury was self-taught and bright, somewhat like Benjamin Franklin, and like Franklin, Ury had ambitions. One from Boston and the other from London, the two young men had come to Philadelphia, then the greatest city in the British North American colonies, to make their way in the world. But, unlike Franklin, who used the Puritan network of his New England home to find patrons, Ury had none. As Franklin admitted in his *Autobiography*, patrons were important to a young man lacking a formal education or family connections. Nor did Ury have Franklin's experience in his brother's printing and newspaper business to give himself a start. Instead, Ury had been a "shop boy" in England with no particular prospects.

Left with nothing except his wits and his learning, Ury reinvented himself as a dissenting divine, patching together bits of theology and pretending to belong to some obscure sect. How he gravitated toward Catholicism is a mystery, but in New York there were enough closet Catholics to support Ury's need to be somebody. Portraying himself as a cleric gave him a special place in their world.

Were it not for the slave plot, Ury might never have come to the attention of the authorities. The city — every city — was full of poseurs and hustlers. Some would become great men, while others would die in obscurity. Ury's fate was different.

The trial itself began on July 29, 1741. Horsmanden regarded his account of the trial of John Ury as especially important. It opened on a fresh page, its title recorded in capital letters — a book within a book. Representing the capstone of the trials, it occupies more space in his account than any that preceded it. All three justices were present in court — a rarity. Horsmanden included minor details, like the colloquy between the clerk of the court and its crier (a kind of bailiff), who called for order in the court. Ury challenged no member of the jury since they came from the middle classes rather than the elite — truly a jury of his peers. Special prosecutors Murray, Alexander, Smith, and Chambers joined Attorney General Bradley for the prosecution. In his defense Ury had only his wits.

The first charge was that Ury counseled Quaco Roosevelt to burn down the fort. Bradley rehearsed all the testimony the grand jury had heard against Ury and promised to disclose the revelations in Oglethorpe's letter about the insinuation of priests into the city. Bradley had one more piece of information — or, rather, prejudice — to share with the jury concerning "that murderous religion" whose emissaries walked among the good people, hiding their secret designs like a cloak of invisibility. Although the charge was fomenting rebellion, Ury's real crime was advocating Catholicism. "For the Popish religion is such, that they hold it not only lawful but meritorious to kill and destroy all that differ in opinion from them, if it may any ways serve the interest of their detestable religion; the whole scheme of which seems to be a restless endeavor to extirpate all other religions whatsoever, but more especially the Protestant religion." The language was straight out of the religious wars of the previous two centuries. Bradley did not mention that Protestants in England had tried to extirpate Catholicism in Ireland, as well as in the Spanish colonies, with or without declarations of war. He also did not note that Catholics lived and (presumably) worshiped in

England and in the other English colonies, notably Maryland. Nor did he remind the jury that Maryland had been founded as a haven for Roman Catholics.

Instead, Bradley laid out the alleged plan of the Catholic Church to subvert and overthrow all other Christian churches: "By subtle argument to persuade the laity out of their senses . . . to get an absolute dominion over the consciences, that they may more easily pick the pockets of credulous people; witness the pretended pardons and indulgences of that crafty and deceitful church." These charges went back to Martin Luther's original indictment of the church in 1517 for the selling of indulgences. How prudent people could be so gulled by doctrines like transsubstantiation — "shocking to the common sense and reason of mankind" — Bradley did not know, but such "blasphemy" could not be allowed to gain a foothold in the colony. The "juggling tricks and . . . bloody" practices of the church that Ury represented must never be allowed to go unpunished. Bradley's assault on Roman Catholicism was hardly probative — it proved nothing about Ury's conduct — and today such prejudicial material would be barred. Had Ury been permitted trained legal counsel, he might have objected to the entire line of argument as irrelevant, immaterial, and prejudicial, but no one spoke up for him.

Bradley had not prepared himself to try the case, and the examination of the first witness for the prosecution was left to Chambers. After a long and lucrative career as a lawyer Chambers would eventually become a judge on the Supreme Court. His first witness was Mary Burton, whose revelations had lost some of their luster. He needed to make her appear as persuasive as possible and spoke to her like a father, urging her to tell the whole story from the beginning, slowly, not "as hastily" as she was wont to do in private. By acting the part of the gentle parent he no doubt hoped to convince the jury that her breathless ebullience should be regarded as youthful enthusiasm. What she had to say was not as important as the way the jury perceived her. The weakness that Chambers saw in her testimony was obvious. Throughout all of April and May and much of June Ury had played no role in her account. All of a sudden, he was not only present but was a dominant figure: catechizing the Hughsons, hearing the slaves' confessions, and boasting that he could forgive Burton's sins as well. He brought with him all the priestly accoutrement, including strange books written in foreign languages she could not understand and chalk to draw circles or other figures on the floor. Indeed, there was something satanic about him, for Satan also spoke in strange tongues and could be summoned by drawing magical shapes on the ground.

The connection between the devil and the Catholics was often made in the colonies, although the New England region was a more likely site for such associations than New York. In 1693 Cotton Mather, one of the leading ministerial authorities on witches and devil worship, claimed that Catholic prayer books were coded versions of demonic liturgies. Supposedly, Mercy Short's exposure to such books during her captivity in Canada, just before the outbreak of the Salem witchcraft trials in Massachusetts, caused all manner of satanic demons to torment her. New York had, in fact, been a haven for some men and women indicted for witchcraft during the Salem episode in 1692–93, but the image of black-robed Jesuits and demons carrying on "extraordinary" rites (in the words of Burton) was present wherever fears of Catholicism thrived.

My own opinion is that Ury pretended to be a Catholic priest but that he did not counsel insurrection — that is, he was not an agent of England's enemies abroad or of the Roman Catholic Church. Instead, making believe that he was a priest made a nobody into a somebody of some unique worth. Since he was not a priest, his ministrations did not pose any political threat to the colony. Nor had he any interest in burning down houses or murdering anyone. He was thus a double victim of his own inadequacies and of the panic that had seized the authorities that summer.

Ury briefly cross-examined Burton. He asked Burton to describe the clothing he usually wore. If he had visited Hughson's establishment so many times, surely she could describe his outfit to the court. She could not, nor could she remember what answer the slaves made when he spoke to them. "I don't remember" was all she could summon. Horsmanden did not display the same interest in Ury's cross-examination that he had demonstrated in the prosecution's case. It is entirely possible that Ury asked additional questions to undermine Burton's credibility. After all, one characteristic Ury possessed that belies the brevity of the historical record is his verbosity. He would not have contented himself with a cross-examination lasting only a few minutes.

Chambers next called William Kane, who swore that he knew Ury well. Indeed, the two men frequented the same locales, attending cockfights, christenings, and taverns. On numerous occasions Ury had tried to persuade Kane to become a Catholic, but Kane had refused. (Horsmanden notes parenthetically that the court believed Kane was a Catholic. This seems a more plausible explanation of why Ury revealed his religious preferences to Kane than Kane's own assertion that Ury was a missionary.) Ury's cross-examination of Kane again focused on his own attire. Kane admitted that Ury did not dress as a priest might. Ury's point was simple: he dressed like an ordinary citizen who held some eccentric religious opinions. He sometimes criticized ministers in the city and occasionally acted in a ministerial capacity, as when he officiated at the now infamous Ryan christening. (In a note added later, Horsmanden identified the child as that of Thomas Ryan, an Irish Roman Catholic servant in the town.) But Ury insisted that nothing he did was out of line with Church of England practices. He never closeted himself with the slaves; all his contact with them was public.

Sarah Hughson Jr., who had been pardoned as a result of her accusations against Ury, now took the stand. To Horsmanden — who had spent pages excoriating the Hughsons' daughter as an obstinate and immoral wretch — she now seemed "composed and decent, touched [with] remorse and compunction." Ury objected to her appearance on the stand. Pardoned or not, she was a convicted felon and could not be sworn in. The court overruled his objection — a questionable step, since her pardon was based on her role in the prosecution of Ury. Ury's real objection was that the pardon was part of a deal to get her to testify against him. Such deals were as common then as now; defense counsels routinely try to convince the jury that the witness's testimony is not only repayment for leniency shown by the court but is perjured.

Sarah Hughson testified that Ury came to her father's tavern late at night; that he made a chalk circle on the floor into which the slaves placed one foot as he absolved them of their sins; that he held up a cross as they swore to him to burn and kill; and that he sought her complicity in the plot. Ury's cross-examination was cursory: he wanted her to identify the object he had used to administer the oath of secrecy. She could not. The language he had used to baptize them was also foreign to her. When asked who was present, she identified Prince Auboyneau, Caesar and Bastian Varick, Quaco Roosevelt, Cuffee Philipse, "and several other Negroes." He did not ask her why her accusation against him was so belated; perhaps he did not know what she had said to the court or when. Today defense counsel is entitled to know what the prosecution knows, which was not then the case.

Murray next spoke for the prosecution, reading the Oglethorpe letter. Ury had no previous knowledge of it either. The prosecution rested. If the jury believed Burton, Kane, and Hughson, it could convict Ury. The prosecution might have made its case stronger by producing at least one slave baptized by Ury. Prince, Caesar, Cuffee, and Quaco had all been executed, but Bastian was still alive and kicking, having been released after pleading his pardon.

Ury's opening address stressed the obvious: Why would he remain at large in New York City where the trials began in May, if he were a part of a conspiracy? He had not yet been named and could have quietly departed the colony. John Romme left, as did Jerry Corker, Fagen, and Plummer (the latter all named as conspirators by Kane). Webb had told Ury that the court was beginning to look askance at him in June. Even then he stayed. He visited Hughson's tavern because his partner, John Campbell, had taken lodgings there. Sarah Hughson was a virago who did not want to lose her room at her father's house to Campbell. When Ury intervened on behalf of his fellow schoolmaster, Sarah used language fit only "for a guardsman."

Ury asked why those slaves whose lives he had supposedly strongly influenced did not name him in their confessions. If (an important "if" to later historians of supposed slave conspiracies), two of the tests of the reliability of a confession were its detail and the corroboration of its details in other testimony, Ury's point was a potent one in his defense. For example, Quaco Roosevelt had not mentioned Ury, though he might have done so to his advantage. "Doubtless he would not have neglected and passed over such a person as I am said to be." Nor had Hughson, his wife, or Peg mentioned Ury.

And why would Ury put himself at risk by revealing his Catholicism to slaves, who never kept a secret, or to "profligate whites" like the Hughsons? Just because he had been seen at Hughson's tavern, did that make him a party to the plot? Many others had been there. Were they also parties to the plot? Up to this point Hughson had been the chief culprit in the eyes of the court. Why suddenly target Ury? In reality, Ury opined, it was the fear of Catholics that had catapulted Ury into the spotlight.

In his defense Ury called John Croker, at whose house he had lodged and whose son he had taught Latin. (Ury had also taught other children to read and write.) Croker gave Ury a good character reference. He had prayed in correct form (for the health of the king) and had never given any evidence of being either an incendiary or a Roman Catholic. Bradley cross-examined Croker to prove that Ury came and went at odd hours — hardly a crime for a free white man. Called by Ury, Webb repeated what he had said to the grand jury, but under cross-examination he owned that Ury had mentioned something about a sacrament day and had sought wafers from DeBrosse. Moreover, Webb had cobbled together a kind of lectern for Ury that, Bradley suggested to the jury, could be used as an altar (although teachers also used bookstands). Of Ury's view of Negroes, Webb said that he believed slaves were "slavish" by nature, a view that might just as well have been ascribed to Aristotle as to a priest and, like the rest of his testimony, neither proved nor disproved Ury's Catholicism. Ury thought that they had souls, but so did Protestant clergymen.

John Campbell testified on behalf of Ury. As far as Campbell knew, Ury had not gone to Hughson's tavern until Campbell tried to take possession of the house. When he did, Hughson's daughter and Ury crossed swords, which might have been her motive for accusing him of complicity in the plot. If the Campbells were to be believed, Sarah could not have known Ury before that time, which would have negated her testimony about his visits before Christmas. Mrs. Campbell also noted that Ury sang psalms, but they were not in Latin or any other foreign tongue.

The Campbells were good witnesses for Ury. Bradley realized that if the jury believed the Campbells, it undermined the conspiracy case against Ury. So the attorney general switched tacks and presented direct evidence on the other charge, namely, that Ury was a priest. In modern criminal trials the prosecution finishes its direct case (that is, presentation of its own witnesses) and rests. Then the defense begins its direct case. The prosecution cannot introduce new evidence after the state's case has been concluded except by special permission of the court (usually to impeach or controvert direct defense testimony). Here the court allowed the prosecution great latitude in bringing forward new direct witnesses.

Bradley called Joseph Hildreth and Richard Norwood. Hildreth was a rival schoolmaster who in February had declined to take on Ury as a partner. Bradley wanted Hildreth to tell the jury about Ury's religious notions. According to Hildreth, when the two met and shared a glass, Ury acted suspiciously, taking out a book and reading from it but snatching it up before Hildreth could glimpse the title page. On another occasion Ury attacked Whitefield's preaching, in the course of which he uttered the phrase "we priests" and defended the Catholic manner of consoling and comforting the sick. Finally, he confirmed that the lectern Webb had sold Ury was actually an altar and that Ury had used it to display the sacrament when he preached. He had told Hildreth that he had a small congregation, but did not invite Hildreth to join. Norwood had some opinions of his own. He had concluded that Ury was "a popish priest." Had he not often arrived late to scheduled lessons with Norwood's children, made "frivolous excuses" by claiming that he had had to visit the sick, and then refused Norwood's request to join him?

Murray, carrying on the prosecution, told the jury that they "must conclude" from the evidence that, "according to the intimation in General Oglethorpe's letter," Ury had been sent as a priest to plot against the colony. William Smith followed this with a series of remarks about the similarity between Ury's practices and the Roman Catholic Church's — for example, in the use of salt in the baptismal rite and the power of the priest to absolve sin. This was clearly not proof that Ury was a priest, that he was sent by some foreign power, or that he acted as an agent of the church in any way. For even if he mimicked the rites of the priests, if he had not been ordained it meant nothing in the eyes of the church, and consequently he had no power to save the sinner. In sum, all the prosecution had proved was that Ury might be a fraud.

Ury based his defense on the absence of proof that he had acted as a priest or was even a priest. There were only unfounded suppositions by those who could not possibly have known what he was doing and had only a vague idea of Catholic practices. The proof was that both Murray and Smith had to read books on Catholic practice to the jury. They had presented no expert witnesses, such as ministers, to testify on the subject. Neither did Ury, but he did not have to prove his innocence; the burden rested on the prosecution to prove his guilt — at least that is where the burden was supposed to rest. In fact, the prosecution's case played as much on the fears of the jurors in the midst of a war against Catholic enemies as it did on anything resembling convincing evidence.

Ury insisted that priests must have confirmation that the person standing before them is actually a Catholic before the priest can offer any of the sacraments. Ury had never asked for or received such assurances, and no one said that he had. For the mass to be celebrated there must be two individuals present at the altar, and no one had alleged this. Nor had he ever demanded penance, a necessary part of confession, of anyone. He might have had missals or other Catholic books in his possession, but that was never proven and, in any case, did not make him a priest any more than Smith's books on Catholic practices made him one.

Ury argued that the state should have been seeking the truth, but his prosecution was based on innuendo and lies. For he was a nonjuring Protestant, and as such he had no love for the oaths of supremacy and allegiance that conformers swore to King George II. In effect, Ury claimed to be the intellectual and spiritual descendant of those Puritans who had risen in rebellion against Charles I. These were the men who had founded New England, and no one was more loyal to the true interests of the home country. As dissenters, they were dangerous to the crown, and that, Ury suggested, was what most concerned Bradley, Smith, and Murray.

Not so, retorted Smith, stung by the accusation and worried that Ury might sway Protestant dissenters on the jury. Realizing that the case against Ury for being a priest had not proved successful, Smith decided to attack the Roman Catholic Church itself, hoping to bring down Ury with a guilt-by-association argument. The Catholic Church was "savage and barbarous," "cruel and unnatural," and through its "contrivance" a "monstrous plot" had been hatched. Smith tried to sway the jury by recalling previous Catholic massacres of Protestants, "the millions of lives, that in remote countries, and different ages, have been sacrificed to the Roman idol," ending in the "blood of our own martyrs." For every massacre there were numerous plots that providence had averted. He insisted that Catholicism could not help itself because of the "destructive tendency of that bloody religion, which, in order to promote its interests, never boggles at the vilest means." Once the jury conceded that the evidence it had heard was "sufficient to produce a general conviction that the late fires in the city, and the murderous design against its inhabitants, are the effect of a a Spanish and Popish plot," then all doubts about Ury would be resolved. Smith's cunning shift from the individual to the general was an appeal to prejudice and fear; he hoped Ury's logic and the flaws in the evidence against him would be overlooked as a consequence. After all, what else could be expected from "those that profess a religion that is at war with God and man"? Priests, he insisted, were trained to lie, to be "artful and cunning" in concealing their activities. The fact that Ury had raised doubts only proved that he was a master of the very skills that every priest possessed. By convicting Ury the jury was in effect convicting the Roman Catholic Church.

The jury took but fifteen minutes to find Ury guilty. He was sentenced to death by hanging two weeks hence (August 15) but was allowed two additional weeks to set his affairs in order. Kane and the others were dismissed, the prosecution having lost interest in them since they had served their purpose. September 24 was declared a day of thanksgiving for the delivery of the city from the plot. The state could forgive as well as punish: on that day Hughson's father and brothers were pardoned on condition that they leave the colony.

CHAPTER 8

Execution According to Sentence

The final stage in the criminal justice process is execution of sentence. Today a minuscule percentage of convicts are executed for their crimes, in large measure because few crimes are still capital offenses. In the eighteenth century capital punishment was much more common because many crimes were still considered capital offenses. The vast majority of capital offenses involved property rather than persons. The punishment for forgery and counterfeiting was a particularly grisly death by burning. The sentence for burglary (breaking into a building at night) and robbery (taking with force) was hanging. In fact, the punishment for grand theft (defined as theft of more than one shilling in English currency) was death. Some of the colonies had rejected this sanguinary code and permitted first-time offenders to escape with branding, jail terms, exile, and paying back triple the value of the thing taken, but the noose was still the common outcome of many criminal careers. It has been estimated that the average white colonist would have seen more than one execution in the space of a lifetime.

Mitigation of sentence after conviction was also possible. The penalty for felony was death, but "benefit of clergy," transportation, pardon, and jury mitigation averted capital punishment for a host of offenses, including burglary. Benefit of clergy was introduced in the fourteenth century to save priests and, later, members of lay religious orders from experiencing the full severity of the law, but by the early eighteenth century benefit of clergy was available for many offenses and could be pleaded by lay men and women as well as clerics. Offenders who were successful might be branded to ensure that they did not plead it for another offense. Colonial courts extended benefit of clergy to some slaves.

In eighteenth-century England capital punishment was also mitigated by "transportation" to the colonies for a term of seven or fourteen years. Transportees were sent to the colonies under guard and placed with masters, who paid for the convict's labor. Upon penalty of death, transportees could not return before their term had expired. Some of these convicts were political dissidents, while others were poor farm laborers who had engaged in some form of protest against their working conditions — for example, by wrecking agricultural machinery or setting crops on fire. The majority of the transportees appear to have been professional criminals, however. Within the colonies, slaves convicted of capital crimes were sometimes sold and transported rather than executed. The value of the slaves as laborers rather than any lenient view on the part of the law determined such mercies. For any slave transported to the West Indies, the sentence was hardly a lenient one since life span for slaves on these islands was usually brief.

Other convicted felons were pardoned by the crown. Upon the request of the home secretary and with the approval of the trial judge, the king issued pardons to over 50 percent of those convicted of capital offenses. Such pardons were purely discretionary, a free gift of the king's grace (or, in the colonies, of the governor's). Its use reaffirmed his authority and emphasized his mercy; the promise of it could be used to turn offenders into informers since the possibility of refusal hung over every unrepentant defendant. Succor from above reminded the convict and the potential wrongdoer that criminal law and the courts were the agencies of the state. Pardons were often granted when the accused confessed to a crime or informed on his confederates. Pardons were always awarded at the discretion of the chief executive, however, and could be withheld at any time and for any reason if he so desired (as some of the slaves soon discovered).

Given all the alternatives available to the court, the number of slaves burned or hanged for participation in the conspiracy may seem excessively harsh. The fact that John and Sarah Hughson, Peg, and John Ury were also executed does not alter this judgment. Although the overall rate of pardon for capital offenses in the New York colony was 51.7 percent, 72 percent of slaves were pardoned in the conspiracy cases. Of 114 slaves who were either convicted or confessed (this figure does not include those individuals arraigned and released or those the grand jury declined to indict), only 31 were executed. If the plot was so heinous, why were so many more pardoned than would have been the case in ordinary capital crimes?

If the conspiracy had involved murder — that is, if the slaves had actually gone on a killing spree instead of merely ranting about revenge — the rate of execution of sentence would no doubt have approached 100 percent. Despite the fulminations of Smith, Bradley, and Horsmanden about the monstrosity of the conspiracy itself, the real crime underlying the conspiracy was the destruction of a handful of properties by a very small number of slaves. After all, the slaves might comprise 18 percent of the population, but the number of adult male slaves involved in the conversation at Hughson's and Comfort's tables was relatively small. True, fire was a terrifying experience for the inhabitants of a tinderbox like New York City, but the actual number of fires during the winter of 1741 — including the ones set by the slaves — was not higher than normal. Accidental fires happened all the time. Moreover, it was only because the fort was set ablaze that the authorities realized the other fires might be the work of arsonists.

Another set of suspicious fires broke out in March 1742. A tannery was set ablaze, and this was followed by hot coals being dumped near Benson's Brewery. Slaves were suspected, but the alderman who interrogated the suspects could not assemble enough evidence to take the cases before a grand jury. Had these fires occurred a year earlier — immediately after the fire at the fort — the investigation would surely have been pressed harder and some of the suspects would have been indicted if not convicted. In the 1741 cases there was no mercy shown for anyone who either set a fire or abetted an incendiary. Only those who were part of the plot and confessed — particularly after the ringleaders had been executed — were granted mercy. It was thus not the crime itself that dictated who would live and who would die.

Plainly, one needs to look more closely at the reasons why the state executed some convicts and remitted the punishment of others. The crucial concept here is that eighteenth-century English and American colonial punishments were all about the display of state power, on the one hand, and the performance of the convicts, on the other. At their intersection lay the reason for the rate of execution. When the slaves confessed, they submitted themselves wholly to the authority of the state. All of the rituals of punishment — including corporal punishments (whipping; confinement in the pillory or "stocks"; and disfigurement, like branding or cropping a body part) and capital punishments (hanging, burning, and dismemberment) — sent a message to the spectators that the state was all-powerful and must be obeyed. If the defendants by their actions had imperiled the state — for example, by setting fire to the fort — they could expect no mercy.

The fort housed the office of the lieutenant governor as well as other offices of colonial government. In the final stages of Ury's trial William Smith told the jury "that Quaco did burn his Majesties' house in the fort. . . . The principal point in this trial, is to prove the prisoner was an accessory to the burning of the king's house in the fort." It was Ury's "public mischiefs" that made his actions so execrable. Horsmanden agreed, for he returned to the fire at the fort, the fire that had set the colony ablaze, in his conclusion to his narrative. Public devastation mattered more than personal damage. The affront to the government was the insult that mattered most, for if the fort could be torched, the entire government was vulnerable. The state executed men, first and foremost, to protect itself — and made sure that everyone knew it.

To reinforce that message, the state resorted to the most gruesome punishments. That was why treason or petty treason was not only punished with dismemberment, but family members of the executed were also punished. By this logic, slaves, who had the least to lose, were made to suffer the most hideous punishments. For example, in mid-September 1739, a week after the battle that ended the Stono rebellion, some thirty or forty rebels were caught trying to reach Florida. They, like their counterparts captured immediately after the fray, were executed and their heads displayed on pikes and poles along the road. On one level, the purpose of the display was to frighten potential rebels and sympathizers, as well as to warn friends and family of the dead not to seek revenge. Similarly, in 1730 when the Dutch militia raided runaway slaves' villages in Surinam as part of the seventy-year-long civil war there, the twelve slaves captured were mutilated and displayed. William Stedman, a Dutch officer, later recalled: "The head shall then be severed and displayed on a stake by the riverbank. . . . The Negro girls . . . will be tied to a cross, to be broken alive, and then their heads severed, to be exposed by the riverbank on stakes." In 1767, for much the same reason, the justices of the peace in colonial Alexandria, Virginia, used the courthouse chimney to display the severed heads of four slaves executed for "petty treason."

The state did not baldly announce that its self-preservation was behind every execution, any more than it admitted catering to the macabre curiosity of the mob. Instead, the judges approached the task of pronouncing the death sentence with a kind of solemn hesitancy. They were not God, who had a plan that encompassed all of life and death and whose judgments could not be questioned. They were simply men, fallible sinners. To condemn others to death they had to speak in a different voice than their own and provide a logic that went beyond the arbitrary exercise of power. The voice was that of the Christian magistrate concerned about the convict's soul. They averred that they took no pleasure in condemning men. It was their duty, both as magistrates sworn to uphold the law and as Christians, to plead with the doomed men to confess their sins and seek the pardon of the Lord. The logic of their position was equally impersonal since the law dictated their actions. The convict had chosen his course; the jury had found him guilty; the law must take its course. Were the logic to be confuted, the entire criminal justice system would lose its rationale.

Yet this facade of judicial impersonality of voice and absence of choice masked the power of the judge to grant mercy. When the judge asked the condemned man to repent before he joined his maker, he did so in order that his soul might be saved, but he also sought something beyond the convict's spiritual awakening. In the 1741 cases some slaves who sincerely repented were nevertheless hanged, while others — like Fortune Wilkins, Jack Comfort, and Bastian Varick — whose demeanor remained cool but changed little, nevertheless gained reprieves. Again, their usefulness to the state as informants was what earned them their lives. The representatives of the state might cast execution in logical and religious terms, but life and death did not depend on the state of the prisoner's soul or the iron logic of the law. Indeed, the more cynical and disloyal the defendant was toward his cohorts, his class, and his race, the more likely it was that he would avoid the noose.

Another kind of display was put on by the defendants. Most condemned men and women were terrified and showed it. Many screamed, moaned, begged for mercy, lost control of their bodily functions, cried incessantly, or went limp, while others became zombies, unaware of anything around them. On other occasions the doomed men and women expressed anger and contempt for the jailers, hangmen, magistrates, and onlookers.

Hughson, who was hanged on June 12, stood in the cart that carried him to the execution ground, looking about as if his rescue were at hand. Though chained, he lifted a hand and beckoned to the onlookers. His wife Sarah "stood like a lifeless trunk," immobile and silent. Peg was animated and bade the sheriff, who presided at all of the executions, to approach, as if she were about to reveal some secrets, but Sarah Hughson intervened and Peg said nothing other than to protest her innocence. All of them had shared a cell for over a month. Half starved, they had lost much of their ability to respond to stimuli.

A woman's behavior on the gallows was quite different from that of her male counterpart. Some men put on a show of calm assurance, insolent swagger, or forced jollity. Like most women, however, Sarah Hughson Sr. refused to perform at all. She had deferred to her husband throughout the trial, only once speaking up to say that they owned no Bible. Her sole expression of emotion was a teary reunion with her youngest child, a suckling babe, brought to her in the dock. According to Horsmanden, she was cold as steel at her execution, where other women fainted or became hysterical.

The authorities wanted the doomed to quietly accept their fate. For the entire process to be successful, the victim had to agree to cooperate. Most of the slaves either refused to say a word or confessed, hoping for a last-minute pardon. Horsmanden commended Wan (Juan de la Silvia) for dying in the right way: "Neatly dressed in a white shirt, jacket, drawers, and stockings," de la Silvia "behaved decently, prayed in Spanish, kissed a crucifix, insisting on innocence to the last" but accepting the awful judgment of the state.

———

The condemned did not always behave as they were supposed to, namely, asking the court's pardon for their crimes and God's pardon for their sins. Some men and women consciously strove to undermine the entire process of execution according to sentence. This contrarian performance might take the form of defiance. Thus, just before he was tied to the stake to be burned alive, Will Ward revealed that he had taken part in other slave rebellions. According to one report in the *Boston Post-Boy* and the *Boston Gazette*, he admitted that he had killed several whites with his own hands.

Another slave used physical demonstrations to denounce his execution. Horsmanden noted that "Walton's [slave] Fortune behaved at the gallows like a mountebank's fool, jumped off the cart several times with the halter about his neck, as if sporting with death." Observers reported to the *New-York Weekly Journal* that he "behaved with such unparalleled impenitence and impudence as to amaze the spectators." Horsmanden recorded that "some conjectured he was intoxicated with rum," which certainly was possible, but another possibility presents itself: it may be that Fortune simply went mad. In other documented cases, particularly when the doomed man had been incarcerated for a long time, he simply lost his wits. There is a third possibility: what looked to the judge like a fool's performance could have been a much more complex, contrived response to an unfortunate fate. Fortune was no fool. As Fortune's master, sea captain Jacob Walton, told the court, Fortune was a busy slave and had little time for gambling and drinking at Hughson's tavern. As best as one could in chains and a halter, Fortune performed a dance of reconciliation and defiance — incomprehensible to white onlookers but recognized by the slaves. It was the same dance that Cuffee had performed outside Philipse's warehouse as it burned down. As the Harlem Renaissance poet Countee Cullen wrote in the 1920s," Come and dance the lover's dance / In an old remembered way." Since dance is capable of expressing all of life's rites of passage through spirited and vigorous movements, it liberates even those in chains and frees those who are on their way to death.

Another tactic used to deny validity to executions was to pray with a little more fervor than the authorities wished. Thus, when some of the men and women of Salem were about to be hanged for witchcraft, they spoke eloquently and movingly of their innocence and commended their souls to God, forcing the magistrates and ministers to restrain the crowd bent on freeing the accused. Protestations of innocence, sincere apologies, heartrending prayers, and quiet dignity also undermined the authority of the execution. In one famous case in 1720, the first man ever executed in Pennsylvania for counterfeiting read a final declaration that turned the tables on the authorities. In the words of historian Michael Meranze, Edward Hunt portrayed himself as "a Christian martyr."

Ury's final address to the people of New York, which he read from the gallows, was another marvelous example of the ritual of execution turned on its head, for Ury went to his death as a martyr to faith. According to the *Boston Post-Boy* of September 7, Ury "kneeled down and prayed very devoutly." Horsmanden reprinted a portion of the speech, in which Ury accepted his fate as the "cup that my heavenly father has placed in my hand, and I drink it with pleasure; it is the cross of my dear redeemer." Likening himself to Christ, Ury prepared to die in a state of glory and trusted in resurrection. God would clear his name and acknowledge his innocence, for only God could pardon the sins of men. He did not wish for a pardon from the lieutenant governor — as if one might ever have been granted. Ury's conscience was clear. He was departing a "howling wilderness" with a "mind serene." His last words were in the form of "advice to you, spectators, will you die as I do, sure of your salvation?" Then he "pulled off his wig," the emblem of his gentle status, and helped place the noose around his own neck. As Ury no doubt fervently hoped all who learned of his fate would remember, the *Boston Post-Boy* emphasized his "composed countenance."

———

Close contact with the condemned was a feature of all early-modern executions. With the exception of a few aristocrats, felons were executed in plain sight of their fellow subjects. The path from the jail to the execution site was the first act in the drama. The condemned rode in a rickety cart, called a timbrel, through the streets to the place of execution, which in New York was located atop a small hill north of the city. Sometimes a clergyman rode inside or alongside the cart and read to the condemned individual from the Bible. The minister would also give a brief sermon at the gallows. N.E.H. Hull has described the scene in her work on serious crime in colonial Massachusetts: "Punishment is the most visible proof of the efficacy of the justice system. . . . Only a few men and women could crowd into the courts to hear a sentence spoken, but many could and did attend the punishments. . . . At this stage of the criminal process the court no longer focused solely upon the individual defendant but on the offense — and all offenses like it. Punishment became an expression of community censure, and the defendant a symbol of disorder, violence, and sin." The sheriff walked or rode in front of the timbrel, with his men escorting the cart. The victim was told to look down during the ride to avoid eye contact with the spectators. The symbolic subtext was the prisoner's recognition that he had already forfeited the benefit of contact with other people and no longer was a member of society. In addition, it demonstrated the submission of the prisoner's will to the awesome power of the law.

According to this version of "dead man walking," every prisoner's facial demeanor was supposed to resemble that of the good slave on the plantation. In the colonies, when African-American and African bondsmen and women were questioned about their activities — particularly when they were suspected of running away — they characteristically had "downcast" eyes. When owners looked slaves in the eye, they had trouble making eye contact. According to the *Virginia Gazette*, Ben, a "light skinned mulatto" who had fled his Virginia master in 1745, had "a down look." Masters also recorded that slaves refused to look at the whip when it was brandished before them. Sometimes the downcast look was a sign that the slave was contemplating suicide. The solemn or serious "down look" was common enough among slaves, but it was not always meant to show shame. The slave might also assume a "roguish" down look or a "sneaking" down look. On the other hand, the slave who looked his master in the eye violated the unwritten rules governing obedience and respect; a slave's continued eye contact with his master implied that he demanded to be treated as an equal. When this became a stare or even a glare, the slave was challenging the very foundations of the institution of slavery. The same held true when the doomed prisoner stared at his jailers or the hangman.

Another reason it was important for the condemned prisoner riding in the timbrel not to look the crowd in the eye was the fear on the part of the authorities that the crowd might try to intervene and rescue the prisoner. Such rescues were rare in the colonies, but there were cases of crowds burning down whipping posts and tearing down jails. There were certainly plots to free prisoners as well. The London mob rioted on a number of occasions when it thought that the condemned were mistreated on the scaffold. No one liked the hangman; in some instances apprentices for the job had to be recruited from among pardoned felons.

Whether or not the condemned gestured to them, like Hughson, or admonished their spirits, like Ury, the crowds pressed in upon the scene from start to finish. Horsmanden was not present at the executions, but he talked to many spectators who were there and he visited the execution site at least once to witness the rotting corpse of John Hughson. Although he may have been squeamish, the offhanded way that he documented the executions — often noting only the names of the victims and the dates — makes it likely that he had no interest in the way that the condemned prisoners died. He was only interested in those confessions that came "in the midst of the flames," which he regarded as the surest evidence of the doomed man's sincerity.

One of the striking silences in Horsmanden's account was exactly what the doomed felt and the crowd saw. Hanging was an extremely painful way to die and could take up to several minutes if performed improperly by the hangman. During that time the victim was slowly strangled. If done correctly, with the weight of the "drop" calculated properly, the neckbone would be broken and death would ensue almost instantly, but if there was too much weight the head was often torn from the body. Sometimes an improperly tied knot slipped behind the head instead of over the Adam's apple, forcing the hangman to pull on the victim's legs to complete the execution. A hood was placed over the victim's head and face to conceal the gross effects of the hanging, but sometimes the hood slipped off and the crowd witnessed the horrifying changes the hanging had wrought. The face grew purple and the tongue protruded; blood mixed with mucus, which dripped from the mouth and nose; and the eyes popped. After the drop, with the head still in the noose, the victim's body convulsed and jerked in all directions as the brain lost oxygen. Urine and feces were ejected as the muscles that normally contained them relaxed.

Death by burning was even more visceral. The victims' clothing burned first, revealing their naked bodies. The excitement of the spectators rose as the crackling of the flames and the screams of the dying man seemed to merge. The smell of burning flesh wafted over the crowd. Death was rarely instantaneous. As a courtesy, some victims were first strangled manually. There is no mention of this act of mercy in Horsmanden's journal. He only notes that Quaco Roosevelt cowered in "great terror" when he stood before the faggots piled beside the stake.

Intended to serve as a moral lesson to the potential sinner, the painful, gory, yet highly sensational executions of the ringleaders actually thrilled the mobs of spectators. Executions became social events, taking their place alongside religious and secular holidays, festivals, parades in honor of visiting dignitaries, or ceremonies to mark the opening of a new legislative session. Everyone who could turned out, including slaves. Several of those who had witnessed the early hangings and burnings would later find themselves in the timbrel on the way to the execution site.

At some hangings the crowd might grow hostile, but apparently the crowd in New York was eager to witness the deaths of the conspirators. Children were present (there was no social convention preventing them from attending) and entire families often came out of sheer curiosity. When the victims dropped or the faggots were set ablaze, a noise rose up from the spectators, like the oohs and aahs that one might hear at a fireworks display. After the event was over, some ghoulish types rushed forward to retrieve souvenirs of the events.

This explains why the authorities permitted three of the slaves' bodies to hang in chains in a public area that few slaves frequented. If the purpose of the punishment was deterrence, the body parts should have been displayed where every slave could see them, as in the aftermath of the 1712 rebellion. Instead, they were displayed where mainly whites could see them, such as public places, where many slaves did not go.

The purpose of public execution of slaves was, in part, to please the crowds with spectacle. Invariably a multitude of whites gathered to watch. In at least one case recorded in New York whites actually prevented the sheriff from effecting a last-minute reprieve of the convicts. The mob turned the execution into a kind of entertainment, a gory circus whose attractiveness increased when the slaves were dispatched in the most grisly fashion and then left to decay on the ropes or in chains. The only comparable event that comes to mind is the Southern lynching party common in the early twentieth century.

V.A.C. Gatrell, who has written the most detailed modern study of spectators at eighteenth-century executions in England, suggests that they provided "secret gratifications" to onlookers that were different from the lessons they were supposed to teach. On the one hand, such executions stimulated spectators' "darker fantasies," which might include sexual or violent images. On the other hand, the frightfulness of the events led some critics to compose lewd and disrespectful parodies of the entire punishment process.

For particularly horrendous crimes, the condemned's bodies were left to rot in chains at the execution site or, in the case of New York, by the riverside. Hughson's rotting corpse confirmed Horsmanden's condemnation of him as a monster. It had turned black — as black as his heart, as black as the evil he conspired to do. For Horsmanden, an educated English barrister, no less than for his more superstitious readers, the verdict of nature was plain. Hughson's worst offense, according to the *New-York Weekly Journal*, was that he was "privy to and promoter of so unparalleled a villainy." In death he had become as black as his evil cohorts in crime. Three years later Horsmanden recalled that "the beholders were amazed at these appearances; the report of them engaged the attention of many, and drew numbers of all ranks, who had curiosity, to the gibbets, for several days running, in order to be convinced by their own eyes, of the reality of . . . wondrous phenomenons." Hughson's body then exploded, discharging "full pails of corruption."

No one claimed the bodies of the executed men and women.

Ordinarily, the family insisted that the dead be properly buried even if the body had been mutilated in the course of execution. There were occasions in England where family members fought with constables when they thought that the corpse was being mistreated. If one believed in the resurrection of the body, it was important that the corpse remain intact. Slaves, under the law, had no families, and in the New York cases the masters evidently did not go to the trouble or wish to incur the expense of removing and interring the bodies of their bondsmen. Other slaves might have intervened, but it was risky, even under cover of night, for them to try to retrieve the bodies for a proper African burial in the Negro burial ground. Sarah Hughson Jr. did not petition for the body of her mother (her father was still hanging in chains). Instead, the sheriff's men probably removed the bodies and buried them in unmarked graves. Ury had "associates" (Horsmanden's term) who, during his final days in jail, took the written version of his speech and published it in Philadelphia. But those associates could not ensure that he would be buried in consecrated ground.

Were the slaves guilty as charged? In other words, did some of the accused slaves conspire to violate the laws of the colony? The answer is yes. One must bear in mind that the law against slave conspiracy was quite broad and encompassed not only Caesar Varick and his larcenous crew, Quaco Roosevelt and the arsonists, but the slaves who had attended the two feasts and complained about their mistreatment. Theirs was merely drunken boasting and angry talk. None of the slaves who swore they would take their masters' lives ever carried out any part of the plan, but under the statute they were considered part of a criminal conspiracy. Even passive listeners like Sandy Niblet were liable under the law. One could reason that the laws dealing with conspiracy conspired against the slaves, treating them in a harsh and discriminatory fashion. In this sense, a number of those convicted of conspiracy were morally innocent.

Were all of the accused guilty? Certainly not. Juries tended not to make fine distinctions, however, particularly when the prosecution refused to try the slaves individually. It was not that in their eyes all blacks looked alike, for some of the jurors knew a number of the accused quite well. Rather, without legal counsel to raise doubts in their minds, point to the inconsistencies in the prosecution's cases, and orchestrate alibis, jurors invariably chose a guilty verdict. Grand juries, however, did exercise more caution — perhaps because suspects were brought before them individually rather than in groups — and refused to indict a number of slaves.

Were the trials a surreptitious means of bringing together the elite and diverting the attention of the free population from class struggle and wartime deprivation? If so, this simply did not work. New York politics continued to roil with partisanship. Class and ethnic animosities would surface in times of crisis, and another war, begun in 1754, would bring even more hardship to the colony. Moreover, there is no evidence to suggest that anyone planned the trials with this covert purpose in mind.

In time the furor subsided. By the end of the summer, the executions had ceased for all but a few cases. These would drag out over the next few years. The Hughsons and Peg were gone, as was

Ury. The other whites that Burton and, later, Kane had named — dancing master John Corry; hatter David Johnson; peddler John Coffin; Irish soldiers Peter Connolly, Edward Kelly, Edward Murphy, and Andrew Ryan — had been discharged. Caesar Varick and his confederate Prince Auboyneau were just bitter memories. Their hanging, along with that of sixteen other slaves, demonstrated the pitiless rigor of the law. Thirteen slaves were burned at the stake, including Quaco Roosevelt, and seventy slaves were sold and sent away — mostly to the West Indies. Seven slaves named in the confessions could not be found, probably having been spirited away by their masters.

On November 4 Mary Burton applied to the common council for her reward as the first person to reveal the details of the plot. A week later, she received eighty-one pounds from the colony for herself and nineteen pounds to pay off the remainder of her indenture. She at least had gained her freedom as a result of her testimony. William Smith Jr. reported rumors that in the last weeks of the trials she had hinted that prominent whites had been behind the plot, and that she had been silenced by the payment. The same sorts of rumors had been reported by Boston craftsman Robert Calef, a critic of the Salem witchcraft trials. He suggested that the young girls who had accused so many women of being witches went too far when they accused the governor's wife of being a witch.

Even the sanguinary punishments of the summer did not defuse Horsmanden's fears, however. After the deportations he had learned that some of the exiled slaves had discussed the plot during the outbound voyage. This may have been more idle, angry talk, but Horsmanden was convinced that "the city and the people were not yet out of danger from this hellish confederacy." He was afraid that not all the conspirators had been rounded up, and the ones still at large "impiously looked upon the oath to be so sacred, that they thought . . . that the eternal welfare of their souls depended upon the strict observance and execution of it."

The end of the year brought "agitation" in Queens and Nassau counties on Long Island, where slaves had formed a militia and marched about "by way of play or diversion," or so they said, but Horsmanden suspected the opposite to be true. They were chastised, but that was all. Horsmanden repeated rumors about slave uprisings in Charleston, whereas in New York, captured Spanish slaves muttered darkly about liberation approaching in the form of a Spanish fleet. Then there was the case of Tom Bradt, the "half-witted" slave of the widow Bradt, who had been caught on February 15, 1742, trying to start a fire in a brewery. He claimed that there was a new conspiracy afoot and named names, but none of the men he named confessed — all had alibis — so only Tom was executed. Yet Horsmanden was not quite done. Lest anyone think his record of the events was "a dream," there was always the stark reality of the fires, "a daily evidence . . . still before our eyes."

For Horsmanden — as for later historians like Herbert Aptheker, Linebaugh, and Rediker — the New York conspiracy was part of a larger pattern of social and racial unrest. The entire Atlantic imperial world, including the European colonies in America and the home countries, seemed to boil over with resentment. Horsmanden would never have conceded that this resentment was the logical response to the oppression of peoples. Instead, he accepted the notion that nature and God had created hierarchies of social and economic status for the good of all. Some races were inferior to others and were therefore meant to serve their betters. Poverty was not a problem to be solved any more than it was the result of an unequal distribution of wealth. It was simply a fact of life. Thus, Horsmanden saw arson purely as the destruction of property and not as a revolutionary act.

Did Hughson think differently? Was he a genuine social rebel? Even the most sincere modern defender of the slaves' resistance to their condition can hardly argue that Hughson opposed the hierarchical system of the city and colony in which he lived. He served alcohol to slaves in violation of a multitude of city and colonial regulations and, worse (at least according to the prosecution), treated slaves as equals, but he never claimed that slavery was evil or that equality was good. Hughson used the slaves just like their owners used them, namely, for his own benefit. Ury may have been closer to an abolitionist, but even his impassioned speech on the gallows stopped short of condemning slavery. Like Hughson, Ury's primary concern was to save himself.

Were the slaves part of a "primitive, radical internationale" — a loose confederation of men who turned to violence to liberate themselves? Some, like Will Ward and the Spanish Negroes, certainly knew about the slave uprisings that periodically ripped through the West Indian colonies. Some expressed their willingness to join in a conspiracy in the hope that they would leave it free men. Others simply had a grudge against an individual, like Quaco Roosevelt. Some, like Sandy Niblet, were coerced into joining, and still others, like Jack Comfort, saw joining the conspiracy as the price of cadging drinks at the "frolicks." Motivations varied, as did conceptions of the ultimate aim of the plot. If the underlying motivation of the ringleaders had been to turn society on its head, the evidence that Horsmanden and the other examiners uncovered did not reveal it. However, this does not mean that the slaves' animosity toward their masters vanished when the conspiracy had been revealed. For all his paranoia, Horsmanden was right: the violent fantasies and conspiratorial mutterings would never cease — not as long as slavery existed.

For Horsmanden's generation of whites, "the daring insolence of Negroes" rankled. No people of color could henceforth be trusted, not because they were oppressed (the court and the prosecution had taken great pains to indicate how lenient slavery in the colony was), but because they came from Africa, and Africans were by nature bestial, impulsive, ungrateful, and untrustworthy. That same message recurred in the colonial newspaper accounts of the conspiracy. As Philadelphia's *American Weekly Mercury* warned on June 11, the aim of the "diabolical scheme" was the destruction of the entire colony, and on June 18 evidence had proved that the "plot has been almost general." A week later the paper reported that slaves were confessing that their plan was to "destroy as many whites as possible." Had the courts been able to uncover evidence of this, many more defendants would surely have been executed, but the nature of rumor is such that it grows more frightening as it spreads. The same panicky language that had distorted the truth in Philadelphia appeared in the *Boston Gazette*, whose readers learned on September 28, 1741, that the plot nearly succeeded in burning down the "entire town."

Meanwhile, the New York City common council and the colonial legislature quickly moved to suppress any further thoughts of resistance within the black community. New laws forbade blacks from fetching water from wells "other than the next well" to their homes on Sundays, when slaves had the day off, thus preventing the assembly of blacks from different neighborhoods at a single well. If they could only draw water from the well nearest them, they could not assemble at some central place on the pretext of drawing water and there plot the next uprising. This applied to the free as well as the enslaved African, revealing the common council's latent conviction that free blacks had been part of the original plot. Blacks were also forbidden to ride about the city or beyond on horseback on Sunday. The law cited its purpose as the suppression of disorderly conduct, but behind the new regulation was the fear that free and slave blacks would use their masters' attendance at church services as an opportune occasion to ride to some secluded spot and there conspire.

When emancipation of the slaves made its way onto the assembly's agenda in the 1780s, the majority wanted to mandate the separation of the races. A draft bill would have forbidden African Americans from marrying whites, giving testimony against whites in court, voting, and holding public office. When emancipation finally arrived in 1799, even its advocates assumed that segregation would be the rule. In the future blacks would not be permitted to board the Hudson River steamboats, to walk along the lanes in Vauxhall Gardens, or to occupy a seat on the new omnibuses that ran up and down the city's avenues. They could find jobs as waiters, coachmen, and servants, but not as merchants or salespersons in the new department stores. Though free, they were still demeaned, part of a segregated society with its own houses of worship, amusements, and mutual aid societies. Even the public almshouse was segregated. In the meantime, New York City people of color had to bury their dead in the old Negro burial ground alongside generations of slaves — the races being separated in death as they had been in life.

Were the trials a turning point in New York's history? Did they alter the development of slave law or the course of empire? Here the verdict is not what one might expect. Although accounts of the trials were carried in colonial newspapers throughout the summer, by the fall the story had vanished. In his history William Smith Jr. concluded that the impact of the trials had remained local. The editor of the 1810 edition of Horsmanden's journal wrote, "The history of the great Negro Plot in 1741, has always been a subject of curiosity, and highly interesting to the citizens of New York." Tradition held that the plot was real enough, but time had shown that "its extent could never have been so great as the terror of those times depicted." Anti-Catholic passions had cooled as well, and the prosecutors' "more favored and enlightened posterity will, therefore, draw the veil of filial affection over the involuntary errors of their forefathers, and emulating their simple virtues, endeavor to transmit a brighter example to their successors." The editor need not have worried. Ironically, the journal itself had become so rare that the editor of the 1810 edition had trouble finding a complete copy of the original 1744 edition to use as the basis for his reprint.

Slavery and slave law spread everywhere in the English colonies, but episodes as disquieting as the New York trials were limited in their geographical and temporal impact. In 1824 Smith opined: "Ought not humanity to revolt at these sanguinary institutions?" Nevertheless he devoted no more than a few pages to the slave trials of 1741. Although later historians deplored the panicky overreaction of the authorities, they still felt that the trials and executions reflected the relative liberality of New York laws. Had not slaves been tried in the same courts as whites? Given the long history of racial abuse and physical mistreatment that slavery entailed, the execution of a few dozen slaves and the exile of seventy or so weighed lightly on the conscience of whites. It was as if slavery's body was so massive that nothing could change its course.

———

What lessons are to be learned from this episode? Some historians believe that the only lesson history teaches is the incapacity of men and women to profit from past experiences. Nevertheless there are important truths to be gleaned from the conspiracy trials. We begin with the idea of conspiracy itself. Even today we are besotted with fears of conspiracy, and our (comparatively) recent history proves how potent those fears can be. The "Red scares" following both world wars, the fear that the Air Force has suppressed evidence of UFOs, the belief in a Jewish conspiracy that controls the media and a Catholic conspiracy that controls the government, not to mention a host of conspiracy theories to explain the assassination of John F. Kennedy — all refuse to go away. The colonists were quick to find conspiracies among the Indians. At the heart of the witchcraft trials in Salem was the conviction that witches in league with the devil had conspired to destroy the colony. Many revolutionaries explained the Stamp Act of 1765 and other imperial tax measures as the product of a parliamentary conspiracy against liberty. The prevalence and the strength of conspiratorial thinking throughout U.S. history suggest that the notion of conspiracy may be basic to our culture. A belief in conspiracies enables people to undersand what otherwise defies explanation. Thus, the fires that appeared in New York City must have been set by conspirators. The thefts of property must have been the work of a ring of thieves. At the root of the whispering of slaves there must have been a plot to destroy the colony.

At the same time that our culture lends itself to fears of conspiracy, it also shapes how we conceptualize conspiracies. We do it in terms of "us" versus "them." The "other"group is different from our group. We rarely regard otherness with complacency or neutrality. Most often we are wary of others, and wariness lends importance to the immediate perception of difference. Our culture is riven with what Erving Goffman, in a seminal essay on labeling, called "stigma-theory." The dangerous other is not quite human — at least not as human as we are — and being different in a society that defines its boundaries by punishing "deviance" magnifies the pain of being an outsider. Sometimes the despised and feared other must wear an identifying symbol, undergo quarantine, or even be eliminated. When the other is recognized through the senses of the observer — by words, dress, facial or bodily features — sensory prejudices trigger a predetermined reading of what we see or hear. The anticipation of the degenerative and debased look, sound, and smell of the other is the self-fulfilling prophecy of prejudice. There can be no doubt that the prosecution in 1741 of so many, so quickly, and upon so little evidence was motivated in part by perceived racial differences. Slaves were considered the "other" by the propertied whites not just because they were laborers but as a result of their skin color and speech patterns. Although the concept of race was hardly as well developed then as now, the prosecution's condemnation of the suspects based on their ethnic origin strongly resembles the racism of American courts in later years. Again the lesson is clear: insofar as the suspected terrorist is demarcated (or "profiled," to use the recent

jargon) by skin color, dress, accent, hairstyle, or other undifferenti-
ated traits, the risk of condemning the individual based on general
stereotypes becomes unavoidable.

One of the purposes of modern criminal procedure is to require
the prosecution to go beyond generalized accusations to prove the
case against individuals. In 1741 the court moved against groups of
slaves rather than against individuals. In no case was a single slave
ever tried in isolation. No one asked for a severance of trials of individual defendants, which is common practice today. In effect, the
court was telling the jurors that all of these men shared the same
general characteristics: they were black; they were slaves; they were
at a certain place at a certain time; and they behaved alike. Thus,
they could be treated as a group.

But that was then, one might object, and this is now. Even the
strongest proponent of swift trials for today's terrorists does not
advocate a return to eighteenth-century English criminal procedure,
much less to freeholders' courts. In fact, the first tribunals following
the disaster of September 11, 2001, did resemble a freeholders' court,
whereas more recent versions offer suspects a defense counsel of
their own choosing, the right to cross-examine, and a presumption
of innocence. At the same time, the model is not the American criminal trial but an abbreviated version of the military court-martial.
Moreover, those men who are acquitted of the charges, like the slaves
reprieved in 1741, will not go free. Slaves remained slaves, and suspected terrorists will remain in custody until "the end of the war"
even if charges against them cannot be proved. When the threat
against U.S. interests appears great enough, we apparently adopt the
mental attitude of the judges and prosecutors at the 1741 trials.

1610s	The first African slaves arrive in English North American colonies.
1661	Barbados introduces the first black code, a comprehensive slave law.
1664	Dutch New Amsterdam is renamed New York City and becomes part of the English colony of New York.
1702	New York slave code is first elaborated; additional provisions follow in 1708, 1709, 1712, 1730, and 1731.
1712	Rebellion of slaves in New York City ends in execution of twenty-five slaves for petty treason.
1730s	Slave insurrections sweep through the West Indies.
1731–1737	A crime wave engulfs New York City. Slaves are suspected of joining gangs of criminals.
September 1739	Stono rebellion occurs in South Carolina, after which hundreds of slaves are executed.
1740–1741	Worst winter in memory in New York City; North (later Hudson) River frozen through spring.
1740–1748	King George's War pits England against Spain.
1741	
February 28	Hogg's shop is robbed, and the Long Bridge Gang is suspected.
March 2	Caesar Varick and Prince Auboyneau are arrested for robbery.
March 4	Mary Burton begins to testify about John Hughson's criminal activities.
March 18	Suspicious fire is set at Fort George, marking a series of arsons in New York City that last from March 25 to April 6.
April 6	Hughson family is detained for fencing stolen goods.
April 11–17	Government officials decide that a conspiracy is behind the fires and offer a reward for information. Cuffee Philipse is arrested.
April 14	Grand jury is convened to hear suspected conspiracy and arson cases; it will sit through August.
April 22	Mary Burton tells the grand jury about the slave conspiracy.

April 23	The court asks leading lawyers for assistance; William Smith, James Alexander, John Chambers, and James Murray agree to serve as special prosecutors and urge the court to require grand jury indictments and jury trials for slaves.
May 1	Caesar Varick and Prince Auboyneau are tried and convicted of burglary; they are sentenced on May 8 and executed on May 11.
May 6	John and Sarah Hughson and Margaret (Peg) Kerry are tried and convicted of feloniously receiving stolen goods; Sarah Hughson Jr. is arrested.
May 12	John Hughson, his wife, and Peg are arraigned for their part in the conspiracy.
May 22	Sandy Niblet begins to reveal all to the grand jury and continues to testify throughout the trials; Fortune Wilkins follows him to the grand jury and also becomes an informant.
May 29	Quaco Roosevelt and Cuffee Philipse are tried for arson, convicted, and burned at the stake on May 30; their attempt to confess is cut short by a mob demanding their execution.
June 1–July 26	Indictments are returned, followed by arraignments of 109 slaves. An additional 33 are committed to jail but are not indicted after examination. Of those committed during this period, 72 confess to playing a part in the conspiracy. Out of a total of 142 slaves examined, 13 are burned at the stake and 18 are hanged.
June 4	The trial of Hughson, his wife, and Peg for their part in the conspiracy concludes. The jury deliberates over the weekend and returns with a guilty verdict on June 8. John and Sarah Sr. and Peg are executed on June 12. Sarah Jr.'s sentence is respited, and she is finally pardoned after her testimony helps convict John Ury.
July 29	The trial of John Ury for his part in the conspiracy and for acting as a Catholic priest ends in his conviction; still averring his innocence, Ury is hanged on August 15.
November 11	Mary Burton is paid for her information in accord with the government's April 17 offer.
1744	Daniel Horsmanden publishes his journal of the trials.

BIBLIOGRAPHICAL ESSAY

A bibliographical essay normally lists the sources an author has consulted. Here it also serves as a guide for further study. Although the 1741 events were long neglected, they have now become the subject of increased attention. As I write, historians Jill Lepore and Serena Zabin are busy completing accounts of the uprising. Peter Linebaugh and Marcus Rediker have featured it in their study of proletarian uprisings in the Atlantic region during the eighteenth century, and Jill Lepore's student Eric Plaag has completed a fine essay on the relation between the Stono rebellion and the events in New York.

The foremost primary source for the story of the conspiracy is Daniel Horsmanden's *Journal of the Proceedings in the Detection of the Conspiracy* . . . , a daily account of the events, first published in 1744 in New York and authored by Horsmanden, identified as "the recorder of the city of New-York." A second edition appeared in 1810 with the new title *The New York Conspiracy.* It was reissued and edited with a new introduction by Thomas J. Davis (Boston, 1971). Horsmanden was a partisan and a protagonist in the story, but the modern editor of Horsmanden's journal believes that the recorder tried to be objective, complete, and fair-minded. I have elected to follow the chronology as presented in Horsmanden's account rather than to excerpt a few of the trials and reorder my account along more analytical lines.

Horsmanden's account is far more detailed than other slave conspiracy transcripts of that era, but one still must resist the temptation to read into it more than it can reveal. There is a tendency to find in slaves' acts far greater meaning than the acts had at the time. Thus a slave's theft of coins becomes not stealing for gain, but a sign of individual autonomy, an act of resistance against the system, a proof of manhood, a symbol of membership in an Atlantic community of proletarian revolutionaries, and an affirmation of the resilience of African identity. All of these larger meanings may be plausible, but the record does not sustain their assertion.

Critical reading of a primary source, even one so voluminous as Horsmanden's journal, is not just an arcane academic exercise. Every time a jury sits at the end of an American trial and tries to sift through the evidence, the men and women on the panel face the identical task. Versions of the same filters — the natural tendency of witnesses to slant their stories to favor their cause, efforts on the part of the counsel for both sides to give the story a particular spin, the rulings that the judge makes regarding the admission of evidence — limit and bias what the jury hears just as the historical record limits what the historian is able to conclude. There is nothing special about the effort to determine if there was a conspiracy — nothing different from the effort of jurors in a modern racketeer-influenced criminal investigation (RICO) trial.

William Smith Jr.'s detailed and judicious account of New York colonial history in this era of partisanship offers wonderful bits of gossip and political insight. A superb modern edition of Smith's history is Michael Kammen, ed., *The History of the Province of New York, Volume One, from the First Discovery to the year 1732 and The History of the Province of New York, Volume Two, A Continuation, 1732–1762, by William Smith, Jr.* (Cambridge, Mass., 1972). For a roster of the players at the mayor's court, see Richard B. Morris, ed., *Select Cases of the Mayor's Court of New York* (Washington, D.C., 1935).

The classic study of criminal procedure in colonial New York is by Julius Goebel Jr. and T. Raymond Naughton, *Law Enforcement in Colonial New York: A Study in Criminal Procedure, 1664–1776* (New York, 1944). They find Horsmanden "gullible" and condemn the trials as a "witch hunt, " a view that Michael Kammen, the leading historian of colonial New York, accepts as well in *Colonial New York: A History* (New York, 1974). The Pulitzer Prize–winning history of the city by Edwin G. Burrows and Michael Wallace, *Gotham: A History of New York City to 1898* (New York, 1998), opines that "the official conspiracy theory cannot be taken at face value." Thus, the journal represents two kinds of primary sources rolled into one: a trial record unique in history, compiled by a contemporary who wanted to assemble every scrap of evidence, and a window into the prejudices of the age. Although the *New-York Weekly Journal* followed the cases as they developed, editor John Peter Zenger admitted that the examinations were not public at the time.

The starting points for the study of slavery in early-modern history are David Brion Davis, *The Problem of Slavery in Western Culture* (Ithaca, N.Y., 1966); Davis, *The Problem of Slavery in the Age of Revolution, 1770–1823* (Ithaca, N.Y., 1975); David Eltis, *The Rise of African Slavery in the Americas* (Cambridge, Eng., 2000); Herbert S. Klein, *The Atlantic Slave Trade* (Cambridge, Eng., 1999); and James Walvin, *Questioning Slavery* (London, 1996).

The literature on slavery in America is too voluminous to be mentioned here; I offer only a sample that focuses on colonial slavery. Prizewinning books on slavery in the colonial era include Ira Berlin, *Many Thousands Gone: The First Two Centuries of Slavery in North America* (Cambridge, Mass., 1998); Rhys Isaac, *The Transformation of Virginia* (Chapel Hill, N.C., 1979); Winthrop D. Jordan, *White over Black: American Attitudes toward the Negro, 1550–1812* (Chapel Hill, N.C., 1968); Philip D. Morgan, *Slave Counterpoint: Black Culture in the Eighteenth-Century Chesapeake and Lowcountry* (Chapel Hill, N.C., 1998); Michael Mullin, *Africa in America: Slave Acculturation and*

Resistance in the American South and the British Caribbean, 1736–1831 (Urbana, Ill., 1992); and Peter Wood, *Black Majority: Negroes in Colonial South Carolina from 1670 through the Stono Rebellion* (New York, 1974).

The literature on resistance and runaways includes Herbert Aptheker, *American Negro Slave Revolts* (New York, 1983); Michael Craton, *Testing the Chains: Resistance to Slavery in the British West Indies* (Ithaca, N.Y., 1972); Philip D. Morgan and George D. Terry, "Slavery in Microcosm: A Conspiracy Scare in Colonial South Carolina," *Southern Studies* 21 (Summer 1982), 121–45; Gerald W. Mullin, *Flight and Rebellion: Slave Resistance in Eighteenth-Century Virginia* (New York, 1972); Jonathan Prude, "To Look upon the 'Lower Sort': Runaway Ads and the Appearance of Unfree Laborers in America, 1750–1800," *Journal of American History* 78 (1991), 127–34; and Peter Linebaugh and Marcus Rediker, *The Many-Headed Hydra: Sailors, Slaves, Commoners, and the Hidden History of the Revolutionary Atlantic* (Boston, 2000).

Slavery in England is the subject of studies by Gretchen Holbrook Gerzina, *Black London: Life before Emancipation* (New Brunswick, N.J., 1995), and Folarin Shyllon, *Black Slaves in Britain* (London, 1974). On the English law of servitude and servants and its carryover to America, see David Galenson, *White Servitude in Colonial America: An Economic Analysis* (Cambridge, Eng., 1981), and Robert J. Steinfeld, *The Invention of Free Labor: The Employment Relation in English and American Law and Culture, 1350–1870* (Chapel Hill, N.C., 1991). In my account of the progressive nature of some portions of slave law, I agree with Deborah Rosen, *Courts and Commerce: Gender, Law, and the Market Economy in Colonial New York* (Columbus, Ohio, 1997), and take issue with the initial premises on contract law presented by Amy Dru Stanley, *From Bondage to Contract: Wage Labor, Marriage, and the Market in the Age of Slave Emancipation* (Cambridge, Eng., 1998), and Morton Horwitz, *The Transformation of American Law* (Cambridge, Mass., 1977). Well before the nineteenth century contracts for the sale of slaves already had a modern structure and appearance and were based on bargained-for exchange.

On the Barbados laws, see Michael Craton, *Empire, Enslavement, and Freedom in the Caribbean* (Kingston, Jamaica, 1997); Richard S. Dunn, *Sugar and Slaves: The Rise of the Planter Class in the English West Indies, 1624–1713* (Chapel Hill, N.C., 1972); and Richard B. Sheridan, *Sugar and Slavery: An Economic History of the British West Indies, 1623–1775* (Baltimore, 1973). David Barry Gaspar has tracked the connections between the Barbados code and its first imitator in Jamaica in " 'Rigid and Inclement': Origins of the Jamaica Slave Laws of the Seventeenth Century" in Christopher H. Tomlins and Bruce H. Mann, eds., *The Many Legalities of Early America* (Chapel Hill, N.C., 2001), 78–96. Peter Charles Hoffer has followed the trail to the mainland colonies in his introduction to Peter Charles Hoffer and William B. Scott, eds., *Criminal Proceedings in Colonial Virginia, The Richmond County Courts Record, 1711–1754* (Athens, Ga., 1984).

On slave law in the mainland colonies and early nation, see Jonathan A. Bush, "Free to Enslave: The Foundations of Colonial American Slave Law," *Yale Journal of Law and the Humanities* 5 (1993), 417–70; Warren M. Billings, "The Law of Servants and Slaves in Seventeenth-Century Virginia," *Virginia Magazine of History and Biography* 99 (1991), 45–62; Thomas R. R. Cobb, *An Inquiry into the Law of Negro Slavery in the United States of America* [1858], ed. Paul Finkelman (Athens, Ga., 1998); and Paul Finkelman, ed., *Race, Law, and American History, 1700–1900*, volume 2, *The African American Experience* (New York, 1992); Daniel J. Flanigan, *The Criminal Law of Slavery and Freedom, 1800–1860* (New York, 1987); Sally E. Hadden, *Slave Patrols: Law and Violence in Virginia and the Carolinas* (Cambridge, Mass., 2001); Oscar and Mary F. Handlin, "The Origins of the Southern Labor System," *William and Mary Quarterly* 3rd ser., 7 (1950), 199–222; A. Leon Higginbotham, *In the Matter of Color: Race and the Legal Process, The Colonial Period* (New York, 1978); and A. Leon Higginbotham and Anne F. Jacobs, " 'The Law Only as an Enemy': The Legitimation of Racial Powerlessness through the Colonial and Antebellum Criminal Laws of Virginia," *North Carolina Law Review* 70 (1992), 969–1069; Peter Charles Hoffer, "Disorder and Deference: The Paradoxes of Criminal Justice in the Colonial Tidewater" in David Bodenhamer and James Ely, Jr., eds., *Ambivalent Legacy: A Legal History of the South* (Jackson, Miss., 1984), 187–201; Thomas D. Morris, *Southern Slavery and the Law, 1619–1860* (Chapel Hill, N.C., 1996); Morris, "Slaves and the Rules of Evidence in Criminal Trials," *Chicago-Kent Law Review* 68 (1993), 1209–40; Philip Schwarz, *Twice Condemned: Slaves and the Criminal Laws of Virginia, 1705–1865* (Baton Rouge, La., 1988); Alden T. Vaughan, "The Origins Debate: Slavery and Racism in Seventeenth-Century Virginia," *Virginia Magazine of History and Biography* 97 (1989), 311–54; Alan Watson, *Slave Law in the Americas* (Athens, Ga., 1989); William M. Wiecek, "The Statutory Law of Slavery and Race in the Thirteen Mainland Colonies of British America," *William and Mary Quarterly* 3rd ser., 34 (1977), 258–80; and Oscar Williams, *African Americans and Colonial Legislation in the Middle Colonies* (New York, 1998). Helen Tunnicliff Catterall, ed., *Judicial Cases Concerning American Slavery and the Negro* (Washington, D.C., 1926), is primarily concerned with the antebellum period but includes some case law from earlier years.

The printed edition of the laws of colonial New York, including those on slavery, are not easily found in a single volume. I have used the original publications reproduced in the Evans collection of Early American Imprints, microfilmed by the American Antiquarian Society. The manuscript record of the Supreme Judicial Court for 1741 that heard the cases no longer exists. A few documents relating to the cases are preserved in Volume 74, folios 32–222, of the Historical Manuscripts of the Secretary of State, at the New York State Archives in Albany. These do not include the April indictments (folios 1–31), but they can be found in the calendar of E. B. O'Callaghan, ed., *Calendar of Historical Manuscripts in the Office of the Secretary of State* (Albany, N.Y., 1866), part 2: 553–55. Almost all of these documents were collected and reprinted in Horsmanden's journal. Brief, untrustworthy, repetitive accounts of the trials appeared in colonial newspapers like the *New-York Weekly Journal*, the *Boston Post-Boy*, *Boston Gazette*, and Philadelphia's *American Weekly Mercury*. These can be found on microfilm at most university research libraries.

On the city and colony, see Patricia Bonomi, *A Factious People: Politics and Society in Colonial New York* (New York, 1971); Burrows and Wallace, *Gotham*; Cathy D. Matson, *Merchants and Empire: Trading in Colonial New York* (Baltimore, Md., 1998); Kammen, *Colonial New York*; Stanley Nider Katz, *Newcastle's New York: Anglo-American Politics, 1732–1753* (Cambridge, Mass., 1968); and Mary Lou Lustig, *Privilege and Prerogative: New York's Provincial Elite, 1710–1776* (Madison, N.J., 1995). Herbert Levi Osgood offers some useful vignettes on the Cosby and Clarke regimes in the second volume of *The American Colonies in the Eighteenth Century* (New York, 1924). The battle over Peter Zenger's fate is discussed in Stanley N. Katz, introduction to *A Brief Narrative of the Case and Trial of John Peter Zenger . . . by James Alexander* (Cambridge, Mass., 1972); Eben Moglen, "Considering Zenger: Partisan Politics and the Legal Profession in Provincial New York," *Columbia Law Review* 94 (1994), 1495–1524; and Paul Finkelman, ed., *A Brief Narrative of the Case and Tryal of John Peter Zenger* (New York, 2000). Colonial historical documents for this period, including Lieutenant Governor George Clarke's 1738 "State of the Province," are collected in E. B. O'Callaghan, ed., volume 4 of *The Documentary History of the State of New York* (Albany, 1851), and New York Common Council, *Minutes of the Common Council of the City of New York, 1675–1776*, volume 5, 1740–54 (New York, 1905). Cadwallader Colden, who watched the events with cynicism, left his letters and papers in good enough order for the New-York Historical Society to publish them in nine volumes from 1918 to 1937; the second volume covers the period from 1730 to 1742, and the third volume from 1743 to 1747.

On deference and its travails, see Charles S. Sydnor, *Gentlemen Freeholders: Political Practices in Washington's Virginia* (Chapel Hill, N.C., 1952), which posited the theme of deference; Rhys Isaac, *The Transformation of Virginia, 1740–1790* (Chapel Hill, N.C., 1979), which polished it; and

Richard Beeman, "Deference, Republicanism, and the Emergence of Popular Politics in Eighteenth-Century America," *William and Mary Quarterly* 3rd ser., 49 (July 1992), 401–30; and Gordon Wood, *The Radicalism of the American Revolution* (New York, 1991), 43–92. For the argument that deference was never what it seemed, or what the elites wanted, see Michael Zuckerman, "Tocqueville, Turner, and Turds: Four Stories of Manners in Early America," *Journal of American History* 85 (1998), 13–42. On deference in the courtroom, see Alan F. Day, *A Social Study of Lawyers in Maryland, 1660–1775* (New York, 1990); Gwenda Morgan, *The Hegemony of the Law: Richmond County, Virginia, 1692–1776* (New York, 1989); William McEnery Offutt, *Of 'Good Laws' and 'Good Men': Law and Society in the Delaware Valley, 1680–1710* (Urbana, Ill., 1995); and A. G. Roeber, *Faithful Magistrates and Republican Lawyers: Creators of the Virginia Legal Culture, 1680–1810* (Chapel Hill, N.C., 1981).

For the New York experience with slavery, see Thelma Foote, " 'Some Hard Usage': The New York City Slave Revolt of 1712," *New York Folklore* 18 (1992), 147–59; Joyce Goodfriend, *Before the Melting Pot: Society and Culture in Colonial New York City, 1664–1730* (Princeton, N.J., 1992); Graham Russell Hodges, *Root and Branch: African Americans in New York and East Jersey* (Chapel Hill, N.C., 1999); James G. Lydon, "New York and the Slave Trade, 1700 to 1774," *William and Mary Quarterly* 3rd ser., 35 (1978), 375–94; and Edgar J. McManus, *A History of Negro Slavery in New York* (Syracuse, N.Y., 1966). Shane White and Graham White's *Stylin': African-American Expressive Culture from Its Beginnings to the Zoot Suit* (Ithaca, N.Y., 1998), traces trends in African-American dress, drawing much of its material from New York City.

On the slave family, see Herbert G. Gutman, *The Black Family in Slavery and Freedom* (New York, 1976). On women's work roles in slavery and freedom, compare Laurel Thatcher Ulrich, *A Midwife's Tale: The Life of Martha Ballard, Based on Her Diary, 1785–1812* (New York, 1991), and Betty G. Wood, *Women's Work, Mens's Work: The Informal Slave Economies of Lowcountry Georgia* (Athens, Ga., 1995). On slaves purchased as mistresses, see Walter Johnson, *Soul by Soul: Life Inside the Antebellum Slave Market* (Cambridge, Mass., 1999), and Judith K. Schaefer, " 'Open and Notorious Concubinage': The Emancipation of Slave Mistresses by Will and the Supreme Court in Antebellum Louisiana," *Louisiana History* 28 (1987), 165–82. Collections of essays on women and slavery include Paul Finkelman, ed., *Women and the Family in a Slave Society* (New York, 1989), and Patricia Morton, ed., *Discovering the Women in Slavery: Emancipating Perspectives on the American Past* (Athens, Ga., 1996).

For a summary of many features of criminal law and some statistical summaries of crime, see Goebel and Naughton, *Law Enforcement;* Douglas

Greenberg, *Crime and Law Enforcement in the Colony of New York, 1691–1776* (Ithaca, N.Y., 1974); Hoffer, introduction to *Criminal Proceedings in Colonial Virginia*; Hoffer, *Law and People in Colonial America*, 2nd ed. (Baltimore, Md., 1998); N.E.H. Hull, *Female Felons: Women and Serious Crime in Colonial Massachusetts* (Urbana, Ill., 1985); and Michael Stephen Hindus, *Prison and Plantation: Crime, Justice and Authority in Massachusetts and South Carolina, 1767–1878* (Chapel Hill, N.C., 1980). Deviance theory is discussed by Kai T. Erikson, *Wayward Puritans: A Study in the Sociology of Deviance* (New York, 1966), and John P. Demos, *Entertaining Satan: Witchcraft and the Culture of Early New England* (New York, 1982).

The 1741 cases themselves have found a dedicated student in Thomas J. Davis. He not only edited the modern edition of the 1810 version of Horsmanden's 1744 narrative but also wrote his own account of the trials in *A Rumor of Revolt: The "Great Negro Plot" in Colonial New York* (New York, 1985). Contrary to the prevalent opinion among historians (whom he cites), Davis believes that there was a conspiracy and that at least some of the slaves were involved. The existence of such conspiracies troubles a number of historians. See Michael P. Johnson, "Denmark Vesey and His Co-Conspirators," *William and Mary Quarterly* 3rd ser., 58 (2001), 915–76, as well as the comments of Edward A. Pearson, Douglas R. Egerton, David Robertson, Philip D. Morgan, Thomas J. Davis, Winthrop D. Jordan, James Sidbury, and Robert L. Paquette, along with the reply of Michael P. Johnson, in "The Making of a Slave Conspiracy, Part 2," *William and Mary Quarterly* 3rd ser. 59 (2002), 135–202. James Sidbury's *Ploughshares into Swords: Race, Rebellion and Identity in Gabriel's Virginia, 1730–1810* (Cambridge, Eng., 1997); Egerton's own *He Shall Go out Free: The Lives of Denmark Vesey* (Madison, Wis., 1999); Pearson's edition of the official record in *Designs against Charleston* (Chapel Hill, N.C., 2000); and Robertson's *Denmark Vesey* (New York, 1999) all rely on official versions of trial testimony. Winthrop Jordan's *Tumult and Silence at Second Creek: An Inquiry into a Civil War Conspiracy*, rev. ed. (Baton Rouge, La., 1995) uses no official record, largely basing itself on the notes of one of the inquisitors, who recorded the confessions of slaves elicited under torture. That apparently sufficed to convince Jordan that a conspiracy had existed. On Nat Turner's Rebellion, see Kenneth S. Greenberg, ed., *The Confessions of Nat Turner and Related Documents* (New York, 1996).

On slaves and arson, see Hindus, *Prison and Plantation*; Mullin, *Africa in America*; and Kenneth Stampp, *The Peculiar Institution: Slavery in the Antebellum South* (New York, 1956).

Whitefield's supposed role in the story is discussed in Peter Charles Hoffer's essay on *The Sensory Worlds of Early America* (Baltimore, Md., 2003). The connection between Catholicism and witchcraft is noted by

Peter Charles Hoffer in *The Devil's Disciples: Makers of the Salem Witchcraft Trials* (Baltimore, Md., 1996). On the controversial issue of gun use in early America, see Michael Bellesiles, *Arming America* (New York, 2000), now the center of much controversy. For contrary evidence, see the forum devoted to his book in *William and Mary Quarterly*, published in April 2002.

On executions, see Vincent Brown, "Spectacular Terror and Sacred Authority in Jamaican Slave Society," paper read at the McNeil Center for Early American Studies, February 22, 2002; V.A.C. Gatrell, *The Hanging Tree: Execution and the English People, 1770–1868* (Oxford, Eng., 1994); Peter Linebaugh, *The London Hanged: Crime and Civil Society in the Eighteenth Century* (London, 1991); Michael Meranze, *Laboratories of Virtue: Punishment, Revolution, and Authority in Philadelphia, 1760–1835* (Chapel Hill, N.C., 1996); and Louis P. Masur, *Rites of Execution: Capital Punishment and the Transformation of American Culture, 1776–1865* (New York, 1989). Capital punishment — for much of the eighteenth century considered the only legally mandated punishment for felony — was gradually cut back in England and America in the following century.

The relationship between the state (or the authorities) and criminals is the subject of many powerful works, in particular Michel Foucault, *Discipline and Punish: The Birth of the Prison*, trans. Alan Sheridan (New York, 1977), and Michael Ignatieff, *A Just Measure of Pain: The Penitentiary in the Industrial Revolution, 1750–1850* (New York, 1978). The argument of many commentators — who take their inspiration from Foucault and Ignatieff — is that innovations like penitentiaries, long seen as "reforms," were in fact simply another, more efficient, means by which the modern state imposed its authority. A seminal text on the labeling of others is Erving Goffman, *Stigma: Notes on the Management of Spoiled Identity* (New York, 1963).

INDEX